WALKING IN CATALUNYA – BARCELONA

MONTSERRAT, MONTSENY AND SANT LLORENÇ DEL MUNT I L'OBAC NATURE PARKS

by Nike Werstroh and Jacint Mig

JUNIPER HOUSE, MURLEY MOSS,
OXENHOLME ROAD, KENDAL, CUMBRIA LA9 7RL
www.cicerone.co.uk

© Nike Werstroh and Jacint Mig 2022
First edition 2022
ISBN: 978 1 78631 077 4

Printed in Singapore by KHL Printing on responsibly sourced paper.
A catalogue record for this book is available from the British Library.
All photographs are by the authors unless otherwise stated.

Route mapping by Lovell Johns www.lovelljohns.com
Contains OpenStreetMap.org data © OpenStreetMap
contributors, CC-BY-SA. NASA relief data courtesy of ESRI

Acknowledgements

We would like to thank the Catalan Tourist Board for their help and enthusiastic support during the research. Thank you to Aicard Guinovart i Marquès, Lluís Santamarta and Pilar Herrero Gomez from the London office for organizing meetings with their local colleagues who then came to meet us at the campsites to share their knowledge about the local areas. Thank you for all the help and tips that you shared with us on these meetings and thanks for all the breakfasts that kept us going on the trails.

Thank you to Joe and Jonathan Williams and everyone from the Cicerone team who believed in this project and worked on this book.

Note on mapping

The route maps in this guide are derived from publicly available data, databases and crowd-sourced data. As such they have not been through the detailed checking procedures that would generally be applied to a published map from an official mapping agency. However, we have reviewed them closely in the light of local knowledge as part of the preparation of this guide.

Front cover: The Sau reservoir and Tavertet cliffs (Walk 13)

CONTENTS

Walk 22 follows shrub-lined paths uphill towards Montserrat Monastery

Updates to this guide

While every effort is made by our authors to ensure the accuracy of guide-books as they go to print, changes can occur during the lifetime of an edition. This guidebook was researched and written during the COVID-19 pandemic. While we are not aware of any significant changes to routes or facilities at the time of printing, it is likely that the current situation will give rise to more changes than would usually be expected. Any updates that we know of for this guide will be on the Cicerone website (www.cicerone.co.uk/1077/updates), so please check before planning your trip. We also advise that you check information about such things as transport, accommodation and shops locally. Even rights of way can be altered over time.

We are always grateful for information about any discrepancies between a guidebook and the facts on the ground, sent by email to updates@cicerone.co.uk or by post to Cicerone, Juniper House, Murley Moss, Oxenholme Road, Kendal, LA9 7RL.

Register your book: To sign up to receive free updates, special offers and GPX files where available, register your book at www.cicerone.co.uk.

Walk 4 climbs towards Salt de Marianegra

Symbols used on route maps

route		P	parking
alternative route		⏢	cave
S	start point	ℹ	tourist information
F	finish point	=	bridge
SF	start/finish point	⌷	refreshment
S	alternative start point	•	other feature
route direction		♜	castle
woodland		🚡	cable car
urban areas			
station/railway			
▲	peak		
⋀	campsite		
■	building		
☗	church/chapel/hermitage		
⬛	monastery		
•	water feature		
✳	viewpoint		

Relief
in metres

1600–1800	
1400–1600	
1200–1400	
1000–1200	
800–1000	
600–800	
400–600	
200–400	
0–200	

SCALE: 1:40,000

0 kilometres   0.5   1

0 miles   0.5

Maps are drawn at 1:40,000 unless otherwise stated.

Contour lines are drawn at 25m intervals and highlighted at 100m intervals.

GPX files for all routes can be downloaded free at www.cicerone.co.uk/1077/GPX.

Walk 27 follows this ledge beside a rock wall

INTRODUCTION

Enjoying the well-deserved panorama from La Mola (Walk 19)

The world-famous architecture, fine restaurants and bustling streets make the city of Barcelona a popular destination. The city undoubtedly has a special vibe and its famous landmarks such as the Sagrada Familia, La Rambla and Parc Güell are visited by millions every year. The Costa Brava has attracted sunseekers for decades but only about an hour from the coastline and Barcelona, the landscape is altogether different.

Fresh mountain streams race down the forested slopes and trails meander up to the highest peaks of Montseny. People – seeking escape from the heat in the summer – have always been drawn to these lush mountains. In the autumn the slopes are dressed in spectacular colours, sweet chestnut trees provide fruits and mushrooms grow beneath the trees. Spring brings fresh colours and perfect temperatures for walking. On a clear day at any time of the year, you can enjoy some grand views from the summits all the way to the Pyrenees.

Lingering legends live among the jagged peaks of the Montserrat range and the iconic monastery with a vertical rock face behind it is the destination of pilgrimages as well as day trips

from Barcelona. The Montserrat range is also dotted with hidden ruins of chapels and hermitages.

The fascinating rock formations provide endless routes for rock climbers but hikers are also spoilt for choice among the labyrinth-like rock needles. There may be a cable car and funicular taking people close to the monastery and higher in the mountains but this magical place is without a doubt best explored on foot. A breathtaking 360-degree panorama greets hikers on the summit of Sant Jeroni, the highest peak in the Montserrat. Take any of the numerous steep narrow trails among the rock needles and it is guaranteed that splendid views will accompany you along the way.

The scenery is dominated by unforgettable rock formations in the St Llorenç del Munt i l'Obac Natural Park. Several scenic routes climb up to the monastery, built on La Mola, the highest peak in the natural park, and a myriad of other trails crisscross the slopes with extensive views towards the Montserrat range and the Montseny Massif. If you travel a bit further, you can follow a section of the long-distance Oliba Trail to the Benedictine monastery of Sant Pere de Casserres near Vic, the capital city of the Osona comarca. Like many other monasteries it was built in a stunning location, overlooking a bend in the river Ter.

Trails skirt around the endless vineyards of Penedès where some of the best quality wines in Catalunya are produced. Steep paths lead to ruins of former castles and watchtowers perched in strategic locations. Some amazing trails also criss-cross the rugged limestone landscape of the Garraf Natural Park. It is so close to Barcelona that you can identify some of the famous landmarks from the summit of La Morella. The region is dotted with caves and chasms surrounded by typical Mediterranean coastal vegetation.

Although proud of its own language and identity, Catalunya has been part of Spain since the 15th century when King Ferdinand of Aragon married Queen Isabella of Castile. The region initially kept its institutions but was then integrated into the Spanish state until the 19th century when a renewed sense of identity lead to a campaign for political autonomy. In 1931, when Spain became a republic, Catalunya was given broad autonomy. However, during Franco's rule (1939–1975) the autonomy was revoked and Catalan nationalism repressed. After Franco's death Spain's restoration of democracy started and in 1979 Catalunya was given a statute of autonomy and recognized nationality. The Catalan language became a joint official language. Recent years have seen some struggles for independence and the political situation can, at times, be complicated.

Catalunya is vast and in this book we only explore parts of the Barcelona province: the Montseny Natural Park, the Montserrat range, Sant Llorenç del Munt i l'Obac Natural Park and some trails in the Guilleries-Savassona

Natural Area as well as the Penedès and the Garraf Natural Park. Most of the trails can be enjoyed all year round and are easily accessible from Barcelona.

Hiking and biking trails are well promoted, and active holidays are encouraged for the growing number of people who want to explore Catalunya beyond Barcelona and the Costa Brava. Some routes and areas might see a great number of hikers and recently there has been a great effort to guide visitors towards the more rural areas of Catalunya. However, you can certainly find quiet, lesser-used trails in each natural park.

Catalunya provides hikers with endless trail options, from easy strolls to more demanding walks. The friendly locals welcome the growing number of people who want to explore these fascinating and diverse areas on foot. Since the pandemic, there is a greater appreciation for the freedom of travel and for less crowded destinations, and many people have rediscovered the simplicity and rewards of hiking.

GEOGRAPHY AND GEOLOGY

Catalunya lies on the Iberian Peninsula, south of the Pyrenees mountain range, with its eastern shores washed by the Mediterranean Sea and its climate shaped by the sea and the mountains. Catalunya consists of four provinces: Barcelona, Girona, Lleida and Tarragona. This book focuses on the Barcelona province. The mountains near Barcelona are part of the coastal Catalan range that was formed in the Eocene when compression contributed to the closure of the Ebro Basin. An extension occurred as the Valencia trough opened up in the Oligocene and Miocene.

The Montseny Massif consists predominantly of schists and other metamorphic rocks such as slate, which have traditionally been used as building material in the Montseny Natural Park. Granite and other intrusive rocks are also present in the area.

The rock formations of the Montserrat range started as sediment on the bottom of the tropical sea millions of years ago. The sea covered central Catalunya for the majority of the Eocene period and dried up about 35 million years ago. The rivers continued to bring sediment to the area and by the beginning of the Oligocene (some 30 million years ago), the layer of sediment was 1000 metres thick. From the pressure and the heat from the earth, the older sediment, buried under the newer sediment, was compacted and cemented until it became rock (conglomerate). About 30–32 million years ago the force that formed the Pyrenees pushed these rocks up with folds and faults. Erosion from water, ice and wind played a significant part in shaping the 'needles' (*agulles*) – the many jagged peaks of the Montserrat.

The Garraf Natural Park is also part of the Catalan Coastal Range and consists of limestone with typical karstified features such as dolines, potholes and limestone pavements.

PLANTS AND FLOWERS

In the Montserrat range, the predominant vegetation is typically Mediterranean, including oak, yew and pine trees and about 1200 different species of shrubs, flowers, grasses and other plants growing on the rocks. Mediterranean evergreen vegetation and holm oak, along with Aleppo pine, are dominant in the Sant Llorenç Natural Park. From early spring a myriad of wildflowers bring fresh colours to the meadows.

The peaks of the Montseny Natural Park are the highest of the Catalan Coastal Range and the altitude and climate provide perfect conditions for a variety of plants and flowers. In the lower areas – the Mediterranean zone – holm (*Quercus ilex*) and cork oaks (*Quercus suber*)

Dwarf fan palm in the Garraf Natural Park (Walk 28)

Holm oaks are the main tree species in most areas (Walk 19)

Rock rose

are dominant. Central European species such as beech, fir, and oak forest populate the slopes between 1000–1500m, and near the summits you can find subalpine meadows. In the springtime you can also see some delicate orchids, such as bee orchids, on the slopes of the Montseny mountains.

The close proximity of the Mediterranean Sea gives ideal conditions for Mediterranean plants; for example, kermes oak (*Quercus coccifera*), rosemary, gorse, butcher's broom, lentisk and strawberry trees in the Garraf Natural Park. Limestone is replaced by sandstone, home to Aleppo pines, in the north-eastern part of the natural park.

WILDLIFE

Alongside many common species that usually exist in the Mediterranean climate and in Central Europe, in the Montseny Natural Park you might see some shy snakes, such as the asp viper, on less-trodden routes.

The only endemic vertebrate in Catalunya is the Montseny brook newt, discovered in 2005. These newts live in seven mountain streams at altitudes of 600–1200m, among beech or oak forests, and it is estimated that there are less than 1500 specimens. The Montseny brook newt is listed as a critically endangered species. The Granota Roja (*Rana Temporaria*), or red frog, is also endangered and can be found near Santa Fe.

The Sant Llorenç del Munt i l'Obac Natural Park is home to over 200 different vertebrates (including wild boar, deer, common genet, different birds of prey, robin, jay, salamander and green snake). The bat population in the caves is also worth mentioning.

Common species found in the Mediterranean climate can be seen in the Montserrat range, including mountain goat, falcon, wild boar and wood pigeon, as well as salamander. The cliffs provide a safe nesting place for the endangered Bonelli's eagle.

The hot and dry conditions in the Garraf Natural Park are great for reptiles like the horseshoe whip snake or the snub-nosed viper, and it's also a good place for bird watching. Among many other species, you might spot black-eared wheatear, rock thrush, ortolan bunting, Dartford warbler, red-rumped swallow, Sardinian warbler and Bonelli's eagle.

You can often spot the impressive griffon vultures (*Gyps fulvus*) flying high above the sheer cliffs near Tavertet in the Guilleries-Savassona Natural Area. These creatures are one of Europe's largest birds, with a wingspan reaching up to 2.8 metres, and are the most social of the four species of vultures in Europe.

For further species check www. iberianature.com.

GETTING THERE

The main train station in Barcelona (Estació de Sants) serves suburban and national as well as international

Several snake species can be found in Catalunya, including vipers

routes. The following websites can help you to plan international routes from European cities:

www.raileurope.com
www.thetrainline.com
www.renfe-sncf.com

The best way to get to Catalunya is to fly to Barcelona and then take the local buses or trains or hire a car to get around.

Barcelona is well connected with other European cities and numerous airlines (including the well-known budget airlines) offer flights from various airports. There are also plenty of direct flights from various UK airports. As always, shop around for the best deals.

If you choose to drive from the UK make sure you have all the right paperwork and insurance for your car and the driver.

GETTING AROUND

Buses

When a bus service is available to or from the trail, especially at either end of a linear walk, it is mentioned in this book. However, buses in rural areas are not frequent and you are strongly advised to check the timetable locally before setting off. If you are planning to get to and from the walks described in this book by buses only, it is highly advisable to seek information at the local tourist office. There may be some on-demand bus services operated (in Montseny and Sant Llorenç Natural Parks).

Trains

From Barcelona there is a train service to many major towns (Monistrol de Monsterrat, Vic, Granollers) located close to the trails. There is also a regular train service along the coast. In most cases you will have to combine train and bus journeys and plan your day carefully. You can find more information at www.renfe.com.

Car

Driving around with a hire car is an easy way to explore this part of Catalunya. Many places and trails are easily accessible by car, and there are usually places to park at the beginning of the trails. If you are planning a linear walk, it might be a disadvantage to have a car parked at one end, but most of the linear walks described in this book are not too long, giving you an opportunity to retrace your steps. However, if you opt to return to your start point, always allow enough time and set off early.

Probably the most convenient place to hire a car is at Barcelona airport on your arrival. You can also find car hire companies in bigger towns but, as always, you can get better deals by booking in advance online. You can find some useful information on the following websites:

www.centauro.net
www.holidayautos.com
www.goldcar.es

The views open up on Walk 5 once you reach the ridge

Taxis

If you want to book a taxi, you can find information about local companies from the local tourist offices and you can also find some useful phone numbers on the following websites:

https://www.montseny.cat/
el-municipi/guia-del-municipi/
com-arribar/
https://santceloni.cat/4740

ACCOMMODATION

Choice of accommodation is always a personal one, taking into account your budget and preferences. There are plenty of hotels and self-catering options to choose from, especially in the coastal areas, and a range of options is available in the bigger towns.

You might opt to tackle several day walks in the same area, or – depending on the length of your holiday – you might consider splitting your time between different bases. If you decide to stay at one base, you can still enjoy different areas as many places are easily reached in a day trip. Make sure you book through a trusted website. When you are looking for accommodation you might want to look at campsites as well, even if you are not planning to sleep in a tent or caravan, as there are several campsites that offer self-catering bungalows. There is a list of campsites in Appendix C.

There is an increased interest in rural tourism and you can check the official guide to tourism establishments in Catalunya on this website: https://establimentsturistics.gencat.cat.

There is also a list of rural houses (*casas rurales*) on the Vallès Oriental Rural Tourism Association's website. However, not every rural house is part of the association, so you might find others as well.

WHEN TO GO AND WHAT TO TAKE

You can almost certainly find a suitable walk in this book for every season. The summer months are hot but the Montseny Natural Park is famously cooler than the coast and Barcelona, and the trails attract day trippers from Barcelona who hope to escape the heat, especially at weekends. Autumn is spectacularly colourful but there might be some rainy days, and there is a very little chance of snow in the winter.

In a similar way the trails can be accessed all year round in the Sant Llorenç Natural Park and Montserrat but the summer heat will be more noticeable as the mountains are lower and there is less vegetation than in the Montseny mountains. Likewise, you might want to avoid the Penedès and Garraf in high summer.

Pack what you would normally take for a day walk. Carry a waterproof jacket, especially in the autumn and winter, and take a warm fleece or jumper to the mountains as it can be cooler on the summits. Comfortable hiking boots, sun cream and sun hat are essential, and always carry ample water, especially in the summer months. Make sure you take your camera to capture the amazing landscapes.

Many of the routes in this guide can be successfully navigated without a map, but it is always advisable to have a map on hand (on paper or digital). Look out for the Alpina maps in the local bookshops or online: www.editorialalpina.com.

LANGUAGE

Most local people are bilingual and speak Catalan as well as Spanish. Most of the signs are in Catalan and also in Spanish, especially in areas popular with tourists. At restaurants the menus are in Catalan as well as in Spanish. If you speak or understand some basic Spanish you will have no problems in the rural areas. English is, however, widely spoken especially among younger people. Appendix D has a glossary of some Catalan and Spanish words that you might find useful.

WAYMARKING

The GR (Gran Recorrido/Gran Recorregut) long-distance trails are marked with white above red stripes and their numbers appear on the signpost – for example, GR 5 or its variations like the GR 5.2 in the Montseny Natural Park. The PR-C (Pequeño Recorrido/Petit Recorregut) trails are usually less than 20km long and are marked with yellow and white and a number such as PR-C 205 (Walk 10).

Waymarkers from different trails

The usually shorter SL-C (Sender Local) trails are marked with green and white, for example, SL-C 122 (Walk 13). Some short local walks are also marked with coloured shapes, like an orange square (Walk 2).

The trails in this book make use of the long-distance trails in the area as well as the shorter PR-C and SL-C routes or a combination of these. The description always mentions what signs you should look out for. Occasionally there are some signs painted on rocks in the Montseny Natural Park or Montserrat or in St Llorenç Natural Park, and it is always pointed out in the description if you have to look out for these. The marked trails usually use an 'X' (in trail colours) to mark the wrong path at junctions. However, if a walk described in this book follows a path marked with an 'X' for a short section (as in Walk 29), it is always mentioned in the description.

The 200km-long GR 5 starts from Sitges, traversing the natural parks of Garraf, Montserrat, Sant Llorenç del Munt i l'Obac, Montseny and the Parc del Montnegre before finishing at Canet de Mar on the coast. It is also known as 'Sender dels Miradores' or 'Senders del Parks Naturals'. There are two variants of the route. The GR 5.1 deviates to Santa Cova and then rejoins the GR 5 in Montserrat, and the GR 5.2 traverses the highest peaks in the Montseny mountain range.

There are some variants of the other long-distance trails in the area. These are always marked with 'GR' followed by the route number and the variant number is added after a dot. Some long-distance trails in the area are also referred to by a name rather than the GR number.

The Oliba Trail (or GR 151) starts from Montserrat and passes through some historic towns and villages with Romanesque architecture before

Looking back towards Garraf on Walk 28

reaching the Pyrenees. It is marked with the familiar GR signs as well as a cross in a circle with a dot in each quarter.

The 106km-long Els 3 Monts route travels through three natural parks, starting from Montseny and finishing in Montserrat. The sign consists of a symbol representing the three mountains and a stage number starting with IP (for example IP-4).

Some of the most popular sections of both the Oliba and Els 3 Monts trails are used for day walks and are often run together with other long-distance trails.

USING THIS GUIDE

The walks in this guide are divided into five sections. Each section begins with a brief introduction to the area and gives some information about potential bases from which to plan your walks.

An information box at the start of each walk provides the following information: start/finish point (including GPS coordinates), length of walk in kilometres, total amount of ascent/total descent in metres, difficulty rating (see the grading information below), the length of time the walk is likely to take, and details about refreshments and access that might be useful to plan your day.

Snack bars, restaurants and springs where you can find drinking water in the mountains are mentioned, but don't rely on them entirely

and make sure you always carry ample water for the day.

Places and features that appear on the accompanying maps are shown in **bold** in the route descriptions.

The times and distances given in the route information boxes and the route summary table are from start to finish of the walk. There are some linear walks described in this book, but in most cases it is possible to retrace your steps or in some cases to take a bus back. However, always check the bus timetable locally or arrange a taxi in advance.

The difficulty of each walk is classified by grade. The grading in this guide is only an indicator; bad weather can make any walk more challenging. Clouds can arrive quickly in the mountains and can leave you with very limited visibility. The grading is:

- **Grade 1:** easy and/or short walk; the trail is without any significant ascent/descent
- **Grade 2:** moderate; medium length or longer walk but mostly on easy terrain
- **Grade 3:** a longer walk and/or more difficult terrain
- **Grade 3+:** more hands-on, requiring some easy scrambling (Walk 5).

The times provided – both for the walks themselves and between landmarks – are approximate. The times given are fairly generous but do not take into account longer breaks for picnics or visiting attractions. Once

21

you have tried some walks using this guide, you will be able to see how your own pace compares to the times given and you can adjust your planning accordingly.

Access to the trails is described in as much detail as possible. To help identify the exact location, GPS coordinates of the start of the trails are also given.

Where a waymarked trail is used, the trail number and the colours of the waymarking/signage are mentioned. Occasionally, the trail described takes an unmarked path or path with a cross 'X', but this is always pointed out in the description.

The book's aim is to introduce some amazing trails in close proximity to Barcelona. There are plenty of other trails in each area, of varying different lengths and difficulty, which aren't in this book.

Appendices

Appendix A contains a route summary table with key information about the walks to help you choose an appropriate route. Appendix B offers some useful contacts and Appendix C lists campsites in the region and provides web links to further accommodation options. A Catalan-Spanish-English glossary can be found in Appendix D.

GPX tracks

GPX tracks for the routes in this guidebook are available to download free at www.cicerone.co.uk/1077/GPX. If you have not bought the book through the Cicerone website, or have bought the book without opening an account, please register your purchase in your Cicerone library to access GPX and update information.

A GPS device is an excellent aid to navigation, but you should also carry a map and compass and know how to use them. GPX files are provided in good faith, but in view of the profusion of formats and devices, neither the author nor the publisher accepts responsibility for their use. We provide files in a single standard GPX format that works on most devices and systems, but you may need to convert files to your preferred format using a GPX converter such as gpsvisualizer.com or one of the many other apps and online converters available.

MONTSENY NATURAL PARK

The panorama unfolds towards the north from the exposed rocks of Esquei de Morou (Walk 2)

Climbing the rocky path to Les Agudes (Walk 1)

MONTSENY NATURAL PARK

The forested slopes of the Montseny mountains are cooler than the coast and many of the trails can be enjoyed almost all year round. Winding roads lead to Santa Fe, a popular starting point for many well-trodden trails (Walk 1, Walk 2). The other trails start from one of the spacious parking areas along the BV-5114 and the GIV-5201 roads or from one of the villages dotted around the mountains. The three highest peaks – Turó de l'Home, Les Agudes and Matagalls – dominate the Montseny Natural Park and there are many rewarding ways to reach these peaks from where you can enjoy some extensive views.

Accommodation can be found in Montseny village, Viladrau or Arbúcies or, if you want to stay in a bigger town, Granollers, Vic or Sant Celoni are not far away. For those who want to stay close to the trails, there are some campsites in Montseny (see Appendix C) or there is also an option to stay at Hotel Sant Bernat, among a few others.

San Celoni, Vic and Granollers can be reached by a regular train service from Barcelona. The Sagalés bus company serves the local areas:

https://www.sagales.com/
https://turisme-montseny.com/en/how-to-get-there/

WALK 1
Turó de l'Home from Santa Fe

Start/finish	Santa Fe, Can Casades. Ample space for parking. N41.773401, E2.462634
Distance	11.5km
Total ascent/descent	610m
Grade	2
Time	4hr
Refreshments	Snack bar at Santa Fe, and a spring on the trail.
Access	Santa Fe is located on the BV-5114 road. There is a bus service from Sant Celoni but check the timetable locally before setting off. Alternatively, you can start this trail from Font de Passavets, located a few hundred metres further north on the BV-5114 road.

This route climbs Les Agudes as well as Turó de l'Home and traverses the ridge between the two highest mountains of the Montseny Natural Park. This route mainly follows the well-trodden PR-C 208 trail, with some fantastic views of the forested mountains of Montseny.

The signposted PR-C 208 trail starts from the large parking area near the restaurant building. Follow the well-trodden path through forest, parallel to the BV-5114 road, for a kilometre.

Reach and cross the BV-5114 road. There is a car park with an information board on the other side of the road. (Alternatively you can start the trail from here, making the route 2km shorter.) The PR-C 208 trail continues from this parking area. Follow the yellow/white stripes and shortly pass **Font de Passavets**. When the path splits go right, across a bridge. (You will return to this junction from the path on the left.) ▶ Ascend on the well-trodden forest path following the PR-C 208 signs. The path crosses a forest track a couple of times, but the route is well

The trail is well signposted with yellow/white stripes and it is very easy to follow.

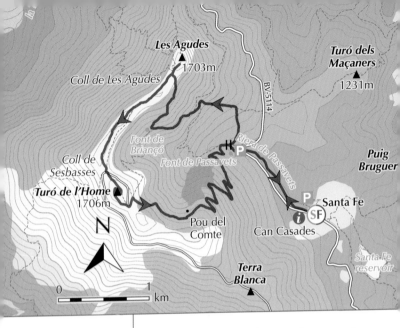

waymarked. About 40min from Font Passavets arrive on a wide forest path. Go left and a few minutes later pass **Font de Briançó** and continue uphill.

Shortly after, the PR-C 208 path splits. The PR-C 208 trail continues to the left towards Turó de l'Home. However, go right (also marked PR-C 208) towards Les Agudes for an extensive panoramic view. Climb the well-trodden path with some views of the forested mountain-sides and about 10min later arrive at a col (**Coll de Les Agudes**) and go right towards Les Agudes (1703m). Climb the rocky path and reach the summit of **Les Agudes** (about 1hr 30min from Can Casades). A 360-degree panorama unfolds. On a clear day there are views of Matagalls, Turó de l'Home and the forested mountains of Montseny.

Retrace your steps to Coll de Les Agudes. Here our route leaves the PR-C 208, initially following the GR 5.2 path heading towards Turó de l'Home. The GR 5.2 then leaves to the right. There is a network of paths here. Follow the ridge with some great views in the direction of Turó de l'Home. Reach a narrow tarmac road (**Coll de Sesbasses**) about 30min after leaving Coll de Les Agudes. Cross the tarmac road and continue uphill on the stony path and a few mins later reach the summit of **Turó de l'Home** (1706m). From the summit you can enjoy a 360-degree panorama, dominated by Matagalls and Les Agudes.

From the summit descend on the PR-C 208 trail marked with yellow/white. Go left behind the building as this section of the trail follows the contour of the top of the mountain allowing you to enjoy further views. Arrive back on the narrow tarmac road near the antennas and information board. Cross the road and go left downhill on the PR-C 208 trail towards Santa Fe. When the path splits go right downhill on the path marked with a yellow/white sign. Every junction is marked with these signs as you descend through beech forest. Every now and then you have a glimpse of Les Agudes. About 20min into the descent pass **Pou del Comte**, a restored ice well. Shortly after pass a smaller ice well. Follow the signposted, well-trodden path downhill. Zigzag downhill and then continue along the stream and arrive back at the car park of Font de Passavets about 40–50min from the ice well and retrace your steps to **Santa Fe**.

Pou del Comte, a restored ice well

WALK 2
Turó de Morou

Start/finish	Santa Fe, Can Casades, N41.773401, E2.462634
Distance	6.5km
Total ascent/descent	270m
Grade	1
Time	2hr
Refreshments	Restaurant/snack bar at the beginning/end of the trail. None along the route.
Access	Santa Fe is located on the BV-5114 road. There is a bus service from Sant Celoni, but check the timetable locally before setting off.

Santa Fe is the starting point for some popular trails in the Montseny Natural Park. Near Can Casades – where an information centre is housed – there is a large picnic area beneath the giant redwoods. This short trail is well trodden and signposted, and offers some fine views of the mountains of Montseny. On the return leg the path skirts around Santa Fe reservoir, created in 1935.

From the BV-5114 road, with Can Casades building and the picnic area on your left, take the track downhill. Before long, notice some route markings – you will be following the trail marked with an orange square. Multiple trails share this section so it is also marked with blue squares as well as PR-C 204 signs. Follow the paved path crossing a stream. Continue straight on, passing a building – **Can Lleonart**.

After Can Lleonart go right on the path marked with the orange square (you might notice another building near the path). When the path splits follow the signs to the right. Shortly after ignore a path on the right and continue straight on, slightly uphill. ◀ When the path splits go left on 'Variant Itinerari al Turó de Morou'. Ignore a path on the left to Coll de la Mosquera, and continue

There are chestnut trees in this part of the forest.

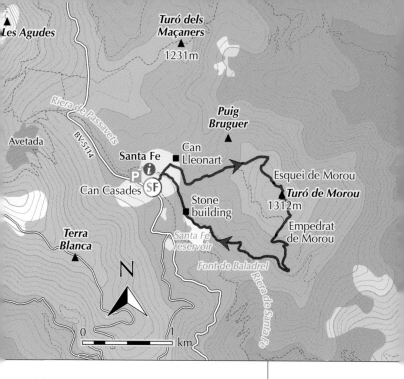

uphill towards Turó de Morou. The path levels out as you walk through the beech forest. About 40–45min after starting the walk, look out for the exposed rocks of **Esquei de Morou** (1290m) on the left-hand side of the path. This is an excellent spot to enjoy the view. The panorama unfolds towards the north, showing the mountains and the rocky face of Les Agudes.

Continue uphill ignoring a faint path on the left. The mountainside is scattered with rocks. The highest point of the trail, **Turó de Morou**, is covered by forest and there are no views from here. Follow the distinguishable path downhill through forest towards Empedrat del Morou. At the junction go left and descend on a rocky path. From **Empedrat de Morou** enjoy extensive views of the ridge between Les Agudes and Turó de l'Home. Continue to descend and at the junction go left. Walk through a

Santa Fe reservoir

section that is partly populated by oak trees with dense undergrowth. Ignore a path joining from the left and carry straight on, shortly spotting the 'La Fageda' sign.

Descend on a rocky path through forest. At the next junction go right joining the PR-C 204 forest path. (You can still see the orange square signs as well.) Ignore a path on the left and follow the wide forest path straight on. Pass a sign marking a path on the left to Font de Baladrel. Carry straight on, passing a house. Notice some boulders near the path. Shortly after pass the dam of **Santa Fe reservoir**. Skirt around the reservoir and pass a **stone building**. As you follow the signs towards Can Casades with the stream down below, look out for a small waterfall on your left near the path. Arrive back at Can Lleonart and retrace your steps back to the **car park**.

WALK 3
Gualba to Santa Fe

Start	Gualba, Plaça de Joan Ragué i Camps, N41.731992, E2.501882
Finish	Santa Fe. Alternatively you can retrace your steps to Gualba.
Distance	9.5km
Total ascent	1060m
Total descent	100m
Grade	3
Time	3hr 30min–4hr
Refreshments	Snack bar in Gualba and a water fountain next to Masia Can Figueres in Gualba at the beginning of the trail. Restaurant in Santa Fe at the end. None along the route.
Access	Gualba is located on the BV-5115 road, accessible from the C-35 road. There is also a bus service from San Celoni to Gualba and it is possible to take a bus back to San Celoni from Santa Fe. However, study the bus timetable carefully before setting off.

Enjoy some scenic views of a deep gorge and forested mountains from this sometimes steep and challenging path from Gualba to Santa Fe. It is worth making the short detour to the Salt del Gorg Negre (waterfall) with its enticing rock pool. This linear route follows the waymarked PR-C 211 trail and can be done as a there-and-back walk if you don't want to rely on the bus service from Santa Fe or if you need to get back to your car.

Leave Plaça de Joan Ragué i Camps by following Passeig del Montseny towards Masia Can Figueres. Continue on Carrer Cami del RACC, pass **Can Figueres** and continue straight on. After 100 metres turn right and follow the road around a small forested park with a stream running through it. After the bridge the road bends left and goes slightly uphill. Follow this towards Parc Mediambiental.

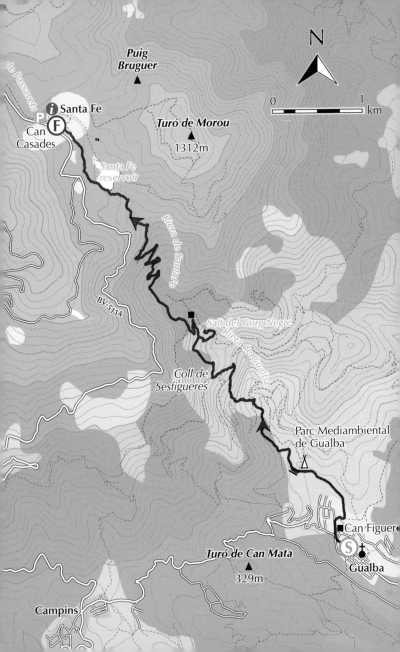

N

Puig
Bruguer

Turó de Morou

1312m

de Passavets

Santa Fe
P
F
Can
Casades

Santa Fe
reservoir

Riera de Santafe

BV-5714

Salt del Gorg Negre

Riera de Gualba

Coll de
Sesfigueres

Parc Mediambiental
de Gualba

Can Figuer

Gualba

S

Turó de Can Mata

329m

Campins

0   1
                  km

This is where you first see waymarkers for this route. Where the PR-C 211 trail splits, go left on the 'Riera de Gualba i Santa Fe pel collet de Sesfigureres' track. (To the right, 'Riera de Gualba i Santa Fe pel Suro Gross' would also take you to Santa Fe, but this is a slightly longer route that climbs on dirt tracks.)

Follow the track passing some houses/villas. Ignore the track marked with a private sign and continue on the wide dirt track. Soon there are some views towards the mountains in front of you. Leaving the houses, pass the entrance of the campsite (**Parc Mediambiental de Gualba**) then cross the bridge and continue on the forest track. Ascend alongside the fence of the campsite. Shortly there is a gorge on your right and there are some views of the mountains across the gorge. At the junction go right uphill with a fence on your right. When the dirt track splits go right slightly downhill, then pass a gate and walk alongside a fence.

Pass Masia Can Figueres

33

Rocks dominate the view above the treeline

Notice some cork oaks near the path as you climb higher. ◄

About 40min after starting from the village leave the dirt track to the left on an uphill path marked PR-C 211 to Santa Fe. This is the beginning of the steep climb. Soon notice a thick water pipe and electricity wire. ◄

Cross a forest track and continue on its other side on a narrow path uphill marked with PR-C 211. About 40–45min after joining this steep narrow path, reach an old pipe at **Coll de Sesfigueres**. Follow the PR-C 211 sign to the left. Walk alongside the old pipeline and electricity posts. The path is level now. When the PR-C 211 trail splits, carry straight on towards Santa Fe. But before continuing to Santa Fe, make a short detour to the Salt del Gorg Negre (waterfall) with a natural rock pool.

Detour to the waterfall
Go right on the narrow path downhill, passing two ruined stone buildings. When the path splits continue straight on to **Salt del Gorg Negre**. (The path on the right continues to Gualba via dirt tracks.) The shore of the natural rock pool is a great spot for a picnic. Allow at least 20–30min for the detour.

Return to the junction where the PR-C 211 splits and go right from the detour, continuing towards Santa Fe. Just before reaching a stone building go left uphill and soon you will hear the sound of trickling water from the right. There is a water pipe along the track. Mountains dominate the view in front of you. The forest track goes beneath a water pipe and then crosses a streambed using rocks (although the streambed might be dry in the summer). Ignore any tracks marked with a yellow/white cross on either side of the forest track. As you ascend you can hear water rushing down over rocks. Shortly – on the right-hand side of the track – you will spot a stream and a small waterfall. Cross the stream using rocks. Leave the track going right and uphill on the PR-C 211 marked path. Reach **Santa Fe reservoir** about an hour after joining the forest track. Continue straight on and follow the PR-C 211 signs to the car park at **Santa Fe** (about 10min from reservoir).

Perfect picnic spot by the rock pool

35

WALK 4
Marianegra spring and waterfall

Start/finish	Area de Les Ferreres car park, N41.802682, E2.434788
Distance	11.5km
Total ascent/descent	560m
Grade	2 (some route-finding difficulties)
Time	3hr 30min–4hr
Refreshments	Refreshing water from the spring at Font de Marianegra.
Access	Les Ferreres car park is located on the BV-5114 road, 5.6km north of Santa Fe.

This route follows meandering tracks through lush forest to a spring. Taste the refreshing water and climb the narrow path marked with rock cairns by the stream. The use of the GPS route provided is highly recommended due to the network of tracks in the area.

From Les Ferreres car park follow the road in the direction of Santa Fe for about 600 metres and look out for a path going downhill on the left-hand side of the road. A rock with **Camí Particular** written on it marks the start of the trail. Leave the tarmac road at this rock, heading downhill. A few minutes later ignore a forest track joining from the left and shortly after another from the right. The path follows the contour of the mountainside. Shortly notice a path on the left-hand side, marked with a rock cairn. This path takes you to a **memorial**, only a few metres off the track, dedicated to the victims of a plane crash (3 July 1970).

Continue on the forest track and when it splits bear left downhill. Ignore a track on the left and follow the contour of the mountainside. At the junction, go left downhill and a few minutes later at the next junction turn right. At the next intersection continue straight on and a few minutes later at the junction turn right on a

DAN AIR FLIGHT 1903

Memorial dedicated to the victims of the 1970 plane crash

On 3 July 1970, after a short flight from Manchester, the Dan Air flight 1903 – carrying 105 holidaymakers and 7 crew – was nearing Barcelona. The Barcelona Approach Control cleared the crew to overfly the Sabadell non-directional beacon and descend to 1800m. As the aircraft made a left turn while descending, the crew reported in error that they had passed the Sabadell non-directional beacon. The Dan Air flight was then instructed to descend to 850m, but as at that time the aircraft was still over the Montseny mountains, the aircraft crashed into trees on the north-east slopes of Les Agudes at 18:05 local time. Les Agudes was in cloud above 760m but visibility was clear below that. The impact destroyed the aircraft and there were no survivors.

After the accident it was said that another aircraft overflew Sabadell at the same time and Barcelona Approach Control mistook that second aircraft's radar echo for the Dan Air flight. However, there is no proof for this theory. This was the most serious aviation accident in 1970. It is believed that the tragedy was caused by a combination of misunderstanding and navigational error. For health reasons the Spanish authorities insisted on the burial of the bodies within 48 hours, and therefore the grieving families from the UK were unable to make their way to the funeral.

forest track. Shortly after ignore the SL-C 84 path on the left. Soon pass a stone building, and when the forest track splits after the house go left downhill. Ignore a path on the right and continue on the forest track with a streambed on your left.

When the forest track splits take the right branch that goes gradually uphill through forest. Ignore a track joining from the right. The forest track winds along the boulder-scattered mountainside. When the track splits take the right branch with old barrier posts slightly uphill and at the junction continue straight downhill on the stony track. Ignore a track joining from the left and continue downhill on a clear stony track. Also ignore an overgrown track on the right and continue to descend, ignoring a track on the left. A ruin of a house appears in front of you about 1hr 10min after starting the walk. Just before reaching the ruined house, turn right on a slightly overgrown track. (At the time of writing this path was covered with cut off branches that had been trampled down.) The towering Les Agudes comes into view.

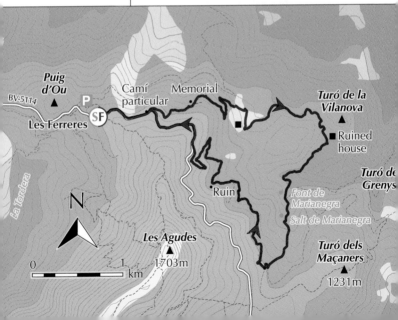

On reaching a forest track go left, and the sound of trickling water accompanies you on this section. Ignoring a track on the left, cross a streambed that goes under the track and continue straight on, slightly uphill. Ignore a track on the right and continue straight on uphill on the rocky forest track. First you will hear the sound of gushing water and soon you will see water rushing down over rocks on your left, in a deep ravine below you. Reach the **Font de Marianegra** where water emerges from four pipes. Fill up your water bottles with this refreshingly cold water.

Walk on a forest track with a streambed on your left

Marianegra spring

After the spring look out for a path going steeply uphill by the stream. Leave the track to the right on this narrow path with the steam on your right. This is a steep climb by the stream passing a small waterfall on your right. Take care as this section can be slippery.

The steep climb by the stream

This section might be a bit overgrown. Look out for rock cairns.

Climb steeply uphill, passing another waterfall (**Salt de Marianegra**) and then ascend with a stream on your right. Look out for rock cairns. Walk alongside the stream and then soon leave the stream and climb uphill. Look out for rock cairns as you zigzag uphill, as the path might be less obvious here. On reaching a forest track, go right. There are some rock cairns along the route. ◄ Ignore two overgrown paths on the left and continue uphill.

On reaching a forest track go right and shortly after leave this track, taking a forest path to the right marked with a rock cairn. The path follows the contour of the mountainside skirting around a gorge. Ignore two tracks on the left and stay close to the gorge on your right. Ignore another track on the right and shortly after also ignore an overgrown track on the left as you descend. Les Agudes comes back into view here. The track crosses a streambed. Ignore a track on the right and, shortly after, a joining track from the left and continue downhill. Pass a ruin with only its fireplace distinguishable. Reach a forest track and go left uphill. Follow the forest track and on reaching the tarmac road, go right and follow the road back to **Les Ferreres car park**.

WALK 5
Les Agudes

Start/finish	Area de Les Ferreres car park, N41.802682, E2.434788
Distance	8.5km or 8km for scrambling route
Total ascent/descent	600m
Grade	3/3+
Time	4hr
Refreshments	Font de Briançó
Access	Les Ferreres car park is located on the BV-5114 road, 5.6km north of Santa Fe.

This is a spectacular route to Les Agudes, the second highest peak in the Montseny Natural Park. It is not signposted; however, there are some painted marks on rocks and surprisingly many people use this path especially on the weekends. The trail described here gives you an option to take a scrambling route, but only choose that option in dry weather. The scrambling route should also be avoided on windy days and when visibility is poor! The alternative route also requires some sure-footedness at places but it is a very enjoyable trail with some amazing views.

From Les Ferreres car park, cross the tarmac road and go uphill on the narrow forest path. Soon you will notice some red marks painted on rocks. About 10min after leaving the tarmac road emerge onto a wider path and go right. (You might notice a narrow path on the right – ignore it. It is a shortcut, and will rejoin this path further up after the bend.) The path bends sharply right, and shortly after this notice the shortcut rejoining from the right. Continue on the narrow forest path uphill with occasional red paint marks. Soon views open up of the mountains on the right and a rocky peak appears in front of you. At the junction go right and shortly after reach a ridge and keep right. The scenery in front of you is still dominated by a rocky peak.

When you reach the forest, notice the faint path on the left-hand side. (You will return down that slightly overgrown path.) Continue uphill following the painted red signs through forest. Shortly after, the path continues on rocks with some views to the surrounding peaks, and then the path runs along a rocky ledge. ◀ Ascend on the rugged path with some towering rocks on the left. Keep right by a rock wall and continue to ascend. Enjoy some great views but take extra care on the tricky terrain. Notice a memorial plaque on the rock face on your left. Shortly after the plaque, reach a narrow section with a big drop on your right. There is a chain here to aid this traverse. The path is distinguishable on the rocks; look out

There are some rock cairns marking the route.

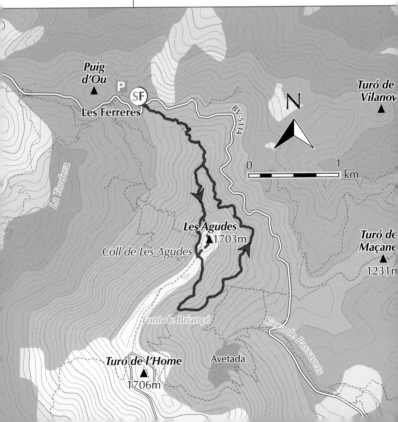

for the painted red signs. There is a short section through woods and then you reach a towering rock. Ignore the painted red signs here and scramble up again following some rock cairns. (The wrong way here takes you steeply downhill through forest and leads to a dead end.) ▶

The faint path goes sharply left and up on rocks. This is the beginning of the scramble up to Les Agudes. Only take this route in dry weather. You will scramble for about 45min on the ridge with some stunning views. This route is only marked with some rock cairns.

If you don't want to take the scrambling route to Les Agudes then continue straight on, ignoring the faint path going sharply left, and a few minutes later reach the GR 5.2 path marked with red/white stripes (1hr 40min from Les Ferreres). Go left uphill with some great views of the mountains. Arrive at **Coll de Les Agudes**, then go left and climb to the summit of **Les Agudes** (1703m).

From the summit descend back to the junction with GR 5.2 sign. (From here it is possible to continue to Turó de l'Home as described in Walk 1.) Go left on the PR-C 208 trail towards Santa Fe (per Briançó).

Views across the valley to Matagalls

You can enjoy some great views.

Uninterrupted views from Les Agudes

Descend following the PR-C 208 signs. At the junction go left downhill (here the PR-C 208 goes right to Turó de l'Home). Shortly after, arrive at **Font de Briançó**.

From Font de Briançó, continue on the PR-C 208 route. A few mins later leave the PR-C 208 path that goes right downhill, and carry straight on. This is an unmarked forest path but you might notice some rock cairns. For a short while the path runs above and parallel to the PR-C 208. When the wide path bends sharply right, leave it to the left on a narrow, slightly overgrown path. There is a rock cairn to mark this path. The path gradually narrows down. Ignore a path on the right and carry straight on. ◀ The path bends sharply left uphill, and you might have to navigate over a fallen tree. One section has ropes attached to the trees and rocks to aid you over slippery ground, but don't rely on these ropes entirely. From time to time the path is a bit overgrown but it is still easy to follow. About an hour from Font de Briançó, arrive on a well-trodden path. Go right and retrace your steps to the **car park** (about 30min from here).

It might be a bit overgrown in places – look out for rock cairns.

WALK 6

Matagalls from Coll de Bordoriol

Start/finish	Coll de Bordoriol, N41.826165, E2.409092
Distance	10km
Total ascent/descent	650m
Grade	2
Time	3hr 30min–4hr
Refreshments	There are some fountains, but these might not provide enough water so always carry ample water for the day.
Access	Coll de Bordoriol is located along the GIV-5201 road, 3.5km north of Coll de Sant Marçal. There are plenty of spaces in the car park.

This is a popular route to the summit of Matagalls, one of the highest mountains in the Montseny Natural Park. The trail described follows the SL-C 82 trail and then a section of the GR 5.2 route as well as some lesser-used paths. Your climb will be rewarded with some extensive views and a 360-degree panorama from the summit of Matagalls.

From the map board in the car park follow the SL-C 82 route, marked with green/white stripes, towards Coll Pregon. Soon pass a path on the right going to Font de Pastors. The track follows the contour of the mountainside. Ignore a turning on the right and shortly after another on the left. Pass a stone building. The well-trodden track is clearly signposted on this section and you can enjoy some views of Les Agudes.

Pass a shrine and go right, towards Matagalls 'per Font de Mosquits'. (The SL-C 82 trail continues on the track on the left, which is the track you will return down.) Shortly after pass **Font de Llops** and then a chain barrier. Ignore a track joining from the right and keep left on the path. About 10min after Font de Llops turn left. Zigzag steeply uphill on the rocky path. The path is easy to follow and marked with rock cairns. Just before reaching the spring, Font de Mosquits, turn left on the narrow path, with a wooden sign: 'Coll Pregon 25min, Matagalls 55min'. (If you carry straight on for a few metres you arrive at **Font de Mosquits**). Ascend with a deep ravine on your right. Zigzag steeply uphill through forest and reach a big forest path junction. Turn right towards Coll Pregon/Matagalls and follow the SL-C 82 signs up to **Coll Pregon**. The junction is marked by a memorial stone with directional arrows on it. Facing this, go right. This section is part of the GR 5.2 trail. Walk along the forested mountainside and, emerging from the forest at a path junction, go right. Ascend on the stony path with some excellent views of the mountains of Montseny. The cross on the peak of Matagalls comes into view well before you reach the summit.

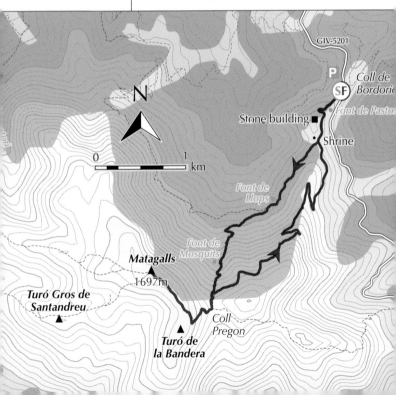

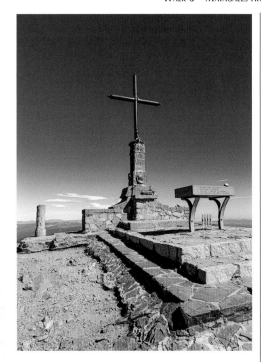

*Creu de Catalunya
(Cross of Catalunya)
on the summit
of Matagalls*

Arrive at the cross on the peak of **Matagalls** (1697m) in about 30min from Coll Pregon. Enjoy the 360-degree views: you can see the two highest mountains, Les Agudes and Turó de l'Home, as well as Viladrau village down below, and on a clear day you can make out the rugged peaks of Montserrat in the distance.

The cross at the top is dedicated to **Mossèn Cinto Verdaguer**, one of the finest poets of Catalan literature. He wrote a poem to honour Matagalls, 'Creu de Catalunya'. According to historical accounts there has been a cross on the top of this mountain since the 17th century. However, the current cross was erected in the 1930s.

Great views towards Les Agudes and Turó de l'Home

The route is well trodden and clear.

From the summit retrace your steps on the GR 5.2 path to Coll Pergon. At the junction with the memorial stone in Coll Pregon go left following the SL-C 82 signs towards Coll de Bordoriol. At the big path junction take the second path from the left. As you descend, soon you have some views towards Viladrau and back towards Matagalls. Descend through forest and soon you can also enjoy some views of Les Agudes. The track then runs along more exposed mountainside. At a junction follow the SL-C 82 sign to the right, and pass an information board about the wildlife in this area. ◄ Ignore a track on the left and follow the signs downhill. About 40–50min from Coll Pregon pass a chain barrier and carry straight on, ignoring the path from your way up to Coll Pregon on the left. Pass a shrine and continue to the **car park** (10min from here).

WALK 7
Sant Bernat to Sant Marçal circular

Start/finish	Hotel Sant Bernat, Montseny, N41.781262, E2.397018
Distance	12km
Total ascent/descent	810m
Grade	3
Time	5hr–5hr 30min
Refreshments	Font Bona de Sant Marçal, restaurant at Sant Marçal, restaurant at Hotel Sant Bernat.
Access	From the BV-5301 road, about 6.5km north from Montseny village.

This trail offers rewarding views from some occasionally steep, lesser-known forest paths, marked only with rock cairns and paint marks. It briefly joins the GR 5.2 and then passes Font Bona de Sant Marçal. The spring provides some excellent-quality drinking water and is a delightful spot to stop for a picnic.

If you are not staying in the hotel then there is a designated parking area near the hotel. Before you start the walk you might want to visit the chapel located in the grounds of Hotel Sant Bernat. You can walk into the garden and find the chapel, built in a neo-romantic style, near the hotel building.

> Both the **hotel** and **chapel** were built in 1952 in a neo-romantic style and were commissioned by the film maker Delmir de Caralt. The buildings are dedicated to Sant Bernat, the patron saint of mountaineers and alpinists.

From the 'Parking Excursionistes' take the track uphill marked 'San Marçal, por Planell y Comellasas' and pass a chain barrier. Ignore a track on the right going to a field and follow the forest track uphill. Pass another chain barrier. Ignore a path on the right (marked with a pink circle

Neo-romantic style chapel in the grounds of Hotel Sant Bernat

and 'Les Illes a San Marçal') opposite **Castañar del Drac**, a very old chestnut tree. Shortly after pass a trail on the left heading towards Sant Bernat and continue straight on uphill. Walk through oak forest and ignore a track on the right. About 15–20min from the parking area, leave the forest track and turn right uphill on a path marked 'Illes'. Ascend here and a few minutes later, just before you start to descend, there is a small rocky peak to the right (**Roca Escanyada**, 987m) from where you can enjoy some views of the Tordera river valley.

As you continue downhill notice some bright pink paint marks. Pass a pipe with dripping water. Notice a wooden sign ('Illes') on a tree. Zigzag downhill on a rocky path marked with some rock cairns. Cross the Riera del Teix **riverbed** and then the path continues uphill, passing a small stone construction.

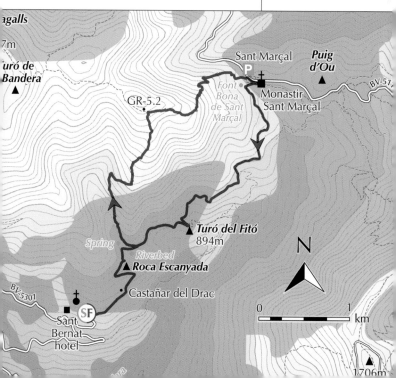

At a junction with wooden signs go left towards Matagalls (you will return on the path on the right). Follow the path uphill and notice some green and bright pink marks painted on rocks. Shortly after, you have some views of the surrounding mountains. Ascend on the narrow path with pink paint marks on rocks. When you notice a wooden 'Font' sign, pointing towards a small spring dripping water a few metres off the path, continue straight on and then zigzag uphill. ◄ The path might be less obvious in places, but the rock cairns will help you to stay on the route.

Look out for rock cairns, painted pink and red marks and painted arrows.

Climb steeply uphill through forest and then follow a rocky path with some views towards Les Agudes and Turó de l'Home. Look out for rock cairns and head towards the treeline. Reach another junction, about 1hr 20min from the junction with wooden signs. Go right, downhill. This well-trodden, clear path is a section of the GR 5.2 trail to Sant Marçal from Matagalls. Zigzag downhill for about 30min following the GR 5.2 signs all the way to Coll de Sant Marçal.

Arriving at **Sant Marçal car park**, walk across the car park and continue downhill on a track signposted to Sant Marçal. Ignore a track on the left (this is the GR 5.2 continuing to Les Agudes and the SL-C 84 to Arbúcies and the Tourdera trail hiker variant). You will be following the Tourdera trail cycle variant for a while.

Follow the track to a small parking area, with the **monastery** and restaurant on the left. Continue on the track downhill and a few minutes later arrive at **Font Bona de Sant Marçal**, the source of the Tordera River. The refreshing cool water is perfect to refill your water bottles.

From the spring continue downhill on the dirt track (Cami de Sant Marçal de Montseny). Shortly after ignore a path on the right. There is a ravine on your left. When the track splits go right, with a 'Tourdera' sign. When the track splits again, follow the Tourdera sign straight on downhill. Notice chestnut trees here. Les Agudes is visible as you descend.

When the track marked with a Tourdera sign turns sharply left, look out for the narrow track on the right.

Go right on this track, slightly uphill at first, and notice a blue paint mark on a tree. Shortly after, as you descend, you can spot some red paint marks on trees. At a junction keep left downhill towards Sant Bernat. After a steep downhill section ignore a track on the left and continue downhill and slightly right. You can hear trickling water and spot a painted pink mark on a tree. Pass a spring – its water runs across the track – and the forest track then zig-zags downhill with some views to Les Agudes.

At a junction go sharply right taking the 'Sant Bernat per Coll Sarrieres' route (ignore the other path to Sant Bernat signed as 'Sant Bernat per Roca Escanyada'). Ignore a path on the right and carry straight on, looking out for painted red marks. The narrow path runs among shrubs and then through forest. ▶ At the junction go left downhill towards Sant Bernat (this was the junction where you went towards Matagalls) and retrace your steps to the parking area near **Hotel Sant Bernat** (25–30min).

Monastir Sant Marçal

There are some giant chestnut trees.

WALK 8
Aiguafreda circular

Start/finish	Aiguafreda, Parc de la Plateria, information point, N41.765790, E2.252445
Distance	16km
Total ascent/descent	420m
Grade	2
Time	4hr 30min
Refreshments	Bars and restaurants in Aiguafreda.
Access	Aiguafreda is about 20km north of Granollers, accessible from the C-17 road.

Follow meandering tracks on the mountainside passing historical landmarks and picturesque landscapes. The trail described follows the signposted PR-C 200 route from Aiguafreda. It is a well waymarked route on easy terrain. The junctions are signposted with yellow/white stripes.

From the information kiosk, keep left and skirt around the playground as the Sant Miquel de Canyelles sign indicates. At the junction continue straight on to Carrer Avencó. Ignoring any side roads, follow this road. A stream (Riera de Picamena) is on your right as you follow this road out of the town. At a junction follow the yellow/white PR-C 200 signs straight on. The tarmac road becomes a dirt track by the Casanova Sant Miquel de Canyelles sign. Pass a sport club on your left, and enter Parc Natural del Montseny.

Follow the dirt track straight on, parallel to the stream, ignoring a dirt track on the left. Pass a storage building. ◄ Cross over a bridge, pass a house, and continue with the stream now on your left. Follow the winding forest track through the river valley with a ravine on your left. Ignore two tracks on the right, and shortly after

Oak trees populate the area near the stream.

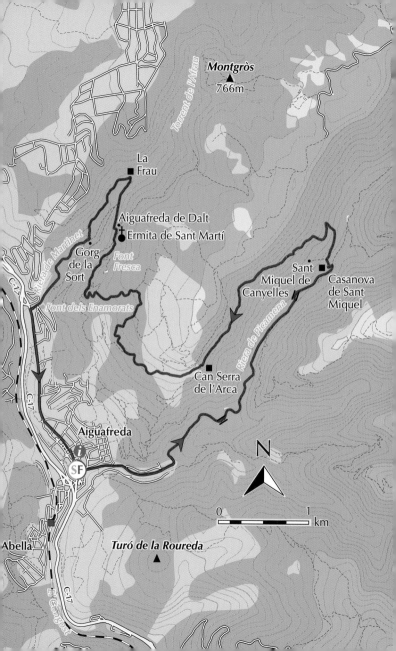

Montgròs
766m

Torrent de l'Arau

La Frau

Aiguafreda de Dalt
Ermita de Sant Martí

Riera de Martinet

Gorg de la Sort

Font Fresca

Sant Miquel de Canyelles

Casanova de Sant Miquel

Font dels Enamorats

Riera de Picamena

Can Serra de l'Arca

Aiguafreda

i
SF

C-17

Abella

La Congost

N

0   1
|_____| km

Turó de la Roureda

Continue on a narrow path after
Can Serra de l'Arca

cross another bridge. Ignore a track joining from the left and follow the yellow/white marks straight on. Soon the views open up towards the mountains.

About an hour from Aiguafreda, at a junction, go left to **Casanova de Sant Miquel**, and shortly after pass the rural hostel and continue steeply uphill. ▶ Reach a path on the left going to **Sant Miquel de Canyelles**; this is an optional short detour to the ruins of a 12th-century church that was built in Romanesque style. As you continue to ascend, you can spot a fire lookout station high up on the nearby mountain.

About 45min after Casanova San Miquel, at the junction, go left slightly downhill (Font del Sami is 780m to the right). You can enjoy further views of the hills as you descend. At the junction with a house (**Can Serra de l'Arca**) go right uphill and a few minutes later leave the dirt track at a bend and continue straight on a narrow path (the GR 2 route continues on the track to the right). This path goes beneath an electricity wire and then traverses the forested mountainside. Notice an old retaining wall in the forest. Arrive on a track and continue straight on. Spot the ruined building on the left with the faint remains of a sundial on its façade. Descend with some mountain views.

Enjoy some great views of tree-covered mountains.

Ruins before reaching Font Fresca

Shortly after, arrive on another dirt track and turn right towards Aiguafreda de Dalt. About 10min later, at the next junction, you can make a short detour to Dolmen de Cruïlles, a megalithic monument that is 50 metres off the route. After returning to the trail follow the yellow/white PR-C 200 signs straight on. At the next intersection go left on the wide path downhill. Follow this rock-paved path ignoring an unmarked path on the right.

At the path junction go left downhill towards Aiguafreda. Follow the yellow/white signs through forest for a few minutes and then arrive at a dirt track. Cross it and continue on its other side. Reach a small forest track and turn right to Aiguafreda. Walk alongside the fence and notice some ruins of a building on the left.

Descend and shortly pass **Font Fresca** and a picnic area, ignoring the path on the right. A few minutes after the picnic area arrive at the old centre of the municipality, Aiguafreda de Dalt, with its church, **Ermita de Sant Martí**.

> The old centre of the municipality of **Aiguafreda** was formed by the old parish church, Ermita de Sant Martí or Sant Martí del Congost, the rectory and some nearby farmhouses. The church dates back to AD898. However, in 1105 it was rebuilt in a Romanesque style and then reconstructed through the centuries.

Go right, passing the church, and descend with some views of tree-covered mountains. Ignore the 'Enllaç itinerari de la riera de Martinet' route on the left and follow the PR-C 200 signs straight on. About 10min from the church cross a stream and turn left, crossing the yard of an artist's house (**La Frau**). Shortly after leave the dirt track to the left on a path towards Aiguafreda. Zigzag downhill on the well-trodden path ignoring any side paths and a few minutes later reach a stream. Cross over on the bridge and arrive at Gorg de la Sort. Notice a small waterfall on the left. Continue with the stream on your right.

At a junction with information boards go right towards Aiguafreda, ignoring any side paths. There are plenty of places where you can stop and rest by the stream. Along the path there are information boards about the vegetation and wildlife of the Martinet river valley. About 15min later reach the tarmac road by Font dels Enamorats and continue straight on. Arrive on a tarmac road by the village sign and turn left. Follow this road all the way back to the centre of **Aiguafreda** (about 15min).

Aiguafreda de Dalt with its church Ermita de Sant Martí

WALK 9

Matagalls from Collformic

Start/finish	Collformic, N41.801068, E2.347328
Distance	11.5km
Total ascent/descent	730m
Grade	2
Time	4hr–4hr 30min
Refreshments	Collformic Restaurant at the start and finish of the trail. Posada el Santuari restaurant at Sant Segimon monastery (check opening hours).
Access	Collformic car park is located on the BV-5301 road.

This scenic route follows the GR 5.2 long-distance trail to the summit of Matagalls where you can enjoy a fantastic 360-degree panorama. Many people use the GR 5.2 trail from Collformic as a there-and-back route to Matagalls; therefore some sections of this approach can get a little busy. From Matagalls there is a steep descent on the PR-C 205 trail with some amazing views.

The trail starts opposite the restaurant building, across the road. A map board and a trail sign mark the beginning of the trail. Go up the stone steps by the map board. Follow the GR 5.2 signs and a few minutes later, at a junction, go left towards Matagalls and Sant Segimon. Go right on the rocky path just before reaching the chain barrier. Ascend the rocky path, soon with some views to Turó de l'Home. You may notice a farm on the right as you ascend. Follow the GR 5.2 signs. At the junction continue straight up on the path marked with GR 5.2 to Matagalls. The track to the left goes to Sant Segimon and you will return to this junction from that track. Ascend on the path, soon passing under a high voltage wire, and then climb among shrubs with views of the nearby barren mountaintops and the valley below.

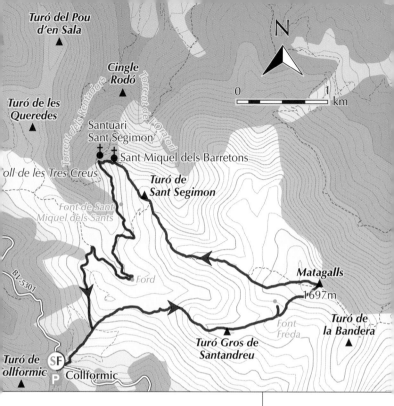

The path levels out for a short section, and you pass an old snow pit on your left here. When the path splits carry straight on, or follow the left branch for a short detour to **Font Freda** then retrace your steps. The sizeable cross on the peak of Matagalls comes into view well before you reach the summit. Reach **Matagalls** summit (1697m) and the 'Creu de Catalunya' (Cross of Catalunya) abut 1hr 30min after starting from Collformic. From the peak you can enjoy an extensive panorama towards the impressive ridge between the two highest mountains in the Montseny Natural Park, Les Agudes and Turó de l'Home. On a clear day you can see all the way to the Mediterranean Sea and make out the rugged Montserrat range and even the silhouette of the Pyrenees.

Views to the barren mountaintops

Facing the cross on the summit take the well-trodden path on your left downhill. With the cross behind you, follow the yellow/white PR-C 205 signs towards Sant Segimon. The path you climbed to Matagalls is visible on the ridge across the valley on your left. You can see the PR-C 205 signs on small green posts as you descend. The path runs along the ridge with some stunning views. Soon walk through a group of trees and then follow a rocky path with views of the nearby mountainsides and the Vic plain in the distance. Pass an information board about 50min from the summit.

About 10min after the information board, notice the 16th-century hermitage of **Sant Miquel dels Barretons** on the right.

Above the Sanctuary of Sant Segimon, at the elevation of 1330m and perched on an exposed rocky outcrop, stands the small hermitage of **Sant Miquel**

dels Barretons, dating back to 1550. *Barretons* means hats in Catalan and the name refers to the legend that a straw hat that cured headaches was kept in this building.

From there follow the yellow/white signs steeply downhill. Head in the general direction of the metal antenna by the dirt track, and look out for signs on the rocks and rock cairns. This is a steep section that can be slippery so take extra care. Arrive at a track and go left. (If you want to visit the **Sanctuary of Sant Segimon**, go right here. It is only a short distance away. After visiting Sant Segimon, return to this junction and continue straight on.) Continue along the track following the contour of the mountainside towards Collformic (about 1hr from here). A deep gorge with the Torrent dels Rentados stream is on your right.

Notice a spring, **Font de Sant Miquel dels Sants**, by the track on the left-hand side. Stay on the track and ignore the path on the left. Walk through a wooded area, and shortly after go through a gate and pass an information board, and then cross a stream at a ford. Shortly after the track crosses the stream again. There are some views of the mountains that you traversed earlier on the way to the summit of Matagalls. Ignore a track on the left and continue towards the electric pylon. Shortly after spot the Collformic restaurant building down below on the right. You can also see a small hut on a hill in front of you, and you can still make out the cross on the summit of Matagalls. Descend on the track and at the junction take the second path on the left towards Collformic (earlier, you took the path on the left to Matagalls) and retrace your steps to the **car park**.

WALK 10

Viladrau to Matagalls

Start/finish	Viladrau town hall, N41.848529, E2.390514
Distance	19.5km (there and back)
Total ascent/descent	1120m
Grade	3
Time	6hr
Refreshments	Cafés/restaurants in Viladrau. Posada el Santuari restaurant at the Sanctuary of Sant Segimon (check opening hours).
Access	Viladrau is located on the GI-520 road.

This steep there-and-back walk to Matagalls requires a whole day, but the effort is rewarded with fine views of the surrounding mountains as well as the Mediterranean Sea and even the Pyrenees. The trail is signposted with yellow/white PR-C 205 signs. During the climb to Matagalls you pass some old farmhouses, hermitages and the Sanctuary of Sant Segimon. Walk through forest and traverse a ridge. On the summit a 360-degree panorama greets you.

Facing the information board in front of the town hall, go right. Follow this street ignoring any joining streets. Carry straight on along Carrer Mercè Torres, pass a church on your left and spot the first PR-C 205 sign just after the church. Go left here (L'Erola Matagalls, PR-C 205). Walk through the village centre where there are cafés, shops and a bakery. In front of the Hostal Bofill Restaurant, go right downhill on Carrer Sant Segimon, and then bear left downhill on Carrer Matagalls. At the end of this road turn right downhill (Carrer Gueran de Liost) and pass a playground. At the roundabout carry straight on, as the sign indicates. Where the dirt track starts, turn right on the narrow signposted path, just after the stone building.

Walk alongside the stream, passing a couple of picnic benches and a **caravan parking area**. Then walk

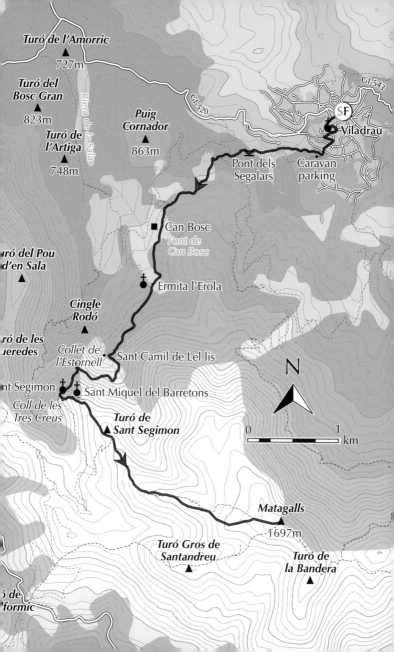

alongside a fence, on your right, and cross over a stream twice using planks. Ignore the path joining from the left and continue straight on (notice the big industrial building on the right). Reach and cross a dirt track and continue on its other side. Ignoring a path on the left carry straight on. ◄ At the junction go left on a small path marked with PR-C 205 sign where other signposted routes carry straight on.

Oak trees populate this area.

Descend through forest with a stream on your left. At a junction near some ruins, carry straight on and cross over a bridge (**Pont dels Segalars**). There are some chestnut trees as you continue straight on slightly uphill, ignoring a path on the right. Notice a building on the right. Carry straight on at the junction and then turn sharply left. When the path splits go right uphill. Walk alongside fields and soon the track narrows down to a path and goes through forest. At the junction carry straight on and then, ignoring a path on the right, follow the yellow/white signs straight on. Notice a small reservoir on the right and a fenced off hole on your left. Arriving on a dirt track, bear left and walk alongside the fence. There are chestnut trees behind the fence.

About 40min from the picnic site at the edge of Viladrau, reach a junction by **Can Bosc** (farm building) and continue straight on, passing further buildings and a spring (Font de Can Bosc) under a stone arch on the left. ◄ After a fenced off area, cross a streambed and pass a reservoir, and then continue uphill ignoring a path on the right.

Towering mountains dominate the scenery.

Reach **Ermita l'Erola**, built in the 16th century, and turn left uphill. Ascend through forest ignoring a path on the right. Admire the mountains and the Sanctuary of Sant Segimon perched on the mountainside. There is a ravine on your right as you follow the contour of the mountain through forest dotted with mighty chestnut trees. As you ascend on the rocky path, views open up towards the valley down below on your right. Pass a shrine called **Sant Camil de Lel lis**. A few minutes later you might hear the sound of trickling water before reaching a stream. Cross this using some rocks and continue uphill with the stream on your left. Ignoring a narrow path on the right continue

constantly uphill on the forested mountainside. This is a steep section.

Arrive at **Collet de l'Estornell**. Go left uphill, but first you can make a short detour to the right to a great viewpoint from where you can enjoy further great views. As you ascend, views open up and you can see Viladrau and the mountains and cliffs of the Guilleries-Savassona Natural Area in the distance. As you walk through forest, you can see Sant Segimon slightly above you on the left. About an hour after Ermita l'Erola emerge onto a dirt track at the **Sanctuary of Sant Segimon**.

The set of buildings at the **Sanctuary of Sant Segimon** were built on the north-west slopes of Matagalls at 1230m between 1636 and 1806, and the church dates back to 1775. Until the Civil War it offered hospitality service for part of the year. It was looted during the Civil War, and restoration started in the 1950s but after finishing the church, due to the difficult access, it was suspended. The restoration work re-started in the 1990s.

The sanctuary and Sant Miquel dels Barretons

Go right towards Matagalls and follow the track for a short distance. Pass a metal triple cross (**Collet de les Tres Creus**), and shortly after, at a bend in the road, leave this dirt track to the left up stone steps towards Matagalls. (The track continues to Collformic, as described in Walk 9.) Climb the steep rocky mountainside. The route is less obvious here, but you can spot some rock cairns and painted marks on the rocks. You can see the sanctuary below and shortly after the ruins of Sant Miquel dels Barretons on the left.

There are some great views all the way to Viladrau and of the beautiful landscape beyond. Follow the rocky path uphill and soon you walk along a ridge with unobstructed views of the mountains and valleys around. The path is more obvious here and easy to follow. At the junction with an information board (Coll Saprunera) follow the PR-C 205 signs straight on uphill on the grassy path. (It is about 40–50min to the summit from Coll Saprunera.)

Soon the cross on the summit of Matagalls is visible. Pass a waymarker at Pla dels Ginebres and a few minutes later, at Collet de Font, follow the yellow/white signs straight on all the way to the summit of **Matagalls** (1697m) with the Creu de Catalunya on top. The cross is dedicated to one of the greatest Catalan poets, Mossèn Cinto Verdaguer. From the summit you can enjoy the extensive panorama of the nearby ridge with the peaks of Turó de l'Home and Les Agudes. The Guilleries-Savassona Natural Area, the rugged peaks of the Montserrat range and the silhouettes of the Pyrenees are also visible on a clear day.

Allow at least 2hr 30min to retrace your steps to **Viladrau**. From Matagalls you can also continue to Coll de Bordoriol, described in Walk 6.

VIC AND GUILLERIES-
SAVASSONA NATURAL AREA

Views of the cliffs of Tavertet (Walk 15)

Views to the sheer rock walls and the reservoir (Walk 15)

VIC AND GUILLERIES-
SAVASSONA NATURAL AREA

There are a great variety of walks in this relatively small area, and in this book we only explore part of this natural area. From Vilanova de Sau walk to a hidden church ruin before climbing to a small rocky peak where you can enjoy some views of the reservoir (Walk 13). The dam was built in 1962 creating Sau reservoir near Vilanova de Sau. The tower of the submerged church of Sant Romà is visible when the water level is low and you can hire a kayak to paddle around it. There might not be high mountains in this area but you can admire almost vertical cliffs near Tavertet and the views are just stunning on every trail. Vic, the capital of the Osona comarca, is well connected to Barcelona and is a good base to explore the area from, with shops, restaurants and accommodation.

From Barcelona, there are regular trains to Vic. From Vic, the Sagalés bus company serves the local area.

WALK 11

L'Enclusa and Castell de Taradell

Start/finish	Taradell, Sant Genis church, N41.875561, E2.285595
Distance	10km
Total ascent/descent	380m
Grade	1
Time	3hr 30min
Refreshments	Cafés and restaurants in Taradell. None along the way.
Access	Taradell is located south of Vic, and is accessible by the BV-5306 and B-520 roads.

Enjoy some amazing views towards Taradell from the peak of l'Enclusa, and explore the ruins of Taradell Castle, the watchtower perched on rocks overlooking Taradell and the surrounding mountains. The trail described is a slightly shorter version of the waymarked PR-C 42 route from Taradell.

Facing Sant Genis church, go right on Carrer de l'Església and then cross the road (Passeig de Domènec Sert) and continue straight on Carrer de l'Església. Cross another road and continue on Plaça d'en Gil then go left of the chapel (there is a fountain in the middle of this small square with a statue), and go left on Carrer de Vic. At the junction keep right downhill ignoring other roads on the left.

Go right on Carrer de la Vilanova (just before the playground). Ignore two roads on the left and one on the right and continue straight on until you reach Ctra. Viladrau (B-520).

Go right on Ctra. Viladrau. At the roundabout go towards Viladrau along the B-520. At the end of the pavement on the left-hand side of the road, just after the last house, look out for the yellow/white PR-C sign. Follow the path parallel to the road for about 100 metres. Yellow/white waymarkers are painted on rocks to show you the way. Ignore any faint unmarked paths.

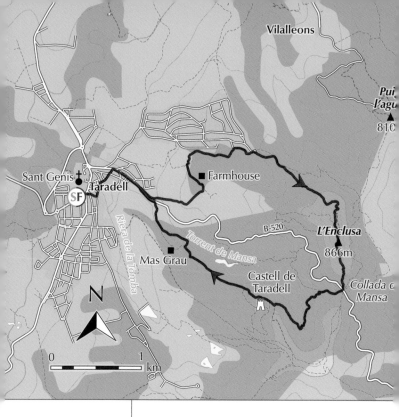

The path bends left uphill among shrubs. Stay on the most prominent path and keep to the right. Walk alongside a field to a rocky platform. Follow the signs as the path bends first right and then soon left. Arrive at a small junction with an information board and go left. Shortly after, at a junction near a farmhouse, take the middle track. Follow the sign and at the next junction go right. Shortly leave the track to the left on the yellow/white waymarked path. Cross a streambed and keep right. There are some houses on your left. Ignore a path on the right and continue straight on. The trail is marked as PR-C 42, Sender de Taradell. Walk alongside a fence and ignore any paths marked with a 'X'. Continue on the marked path uphill.

As you pass some houses the first views of the distant mountains appear over the trees. Just before you reach a small tarmac road with a roundabout near a house, go right. This is a wide rocky trail with some excellent views from the rocky ledge on its right-hand side. Reach a dirt track and go right. At the junction with signposts take the PR-C 42 route to the right heading uphill. Ignore any unmarked paths and paths marked with an 'X', and follow the yellow/white signs. As you ascend the well-trodden path, there are views of the plain below as well as of the distant hills and mountains. When the path gets closer to the jagged rocky ledge there are far-reaching views on your left; on a clear day you can make out the silhouettes of Les Agudes and Matagalls in the Montseny Massif.

About 30–40min after leaving the dirt track arrive at a junction with signposts. The PR-C 42 heads downhill to the left skipping the summit of l'Enclusa entirely. Deviating from the PR-C 42, continue straight on towards l'Enclusa. Reach a wide path and go left uphill. Pass an antenna and shortly after, a trig point. This narrow rocky outcrop at the end of the ridge is shaped like an anvil,

Views of Les Agudes and Matagalls in the Montseny Massif

hence the name **l'Enclusa** (The Anvil). At 866m this is the highest point but the views are better a little further on. Descend slightly – there is a network of paths here – and head towards the flag.

Enjoy the great panorama from this outcrop with the flagpole. It is a perfect spot for a picnic. You can spot the tower of Sant Genis church in Taradell and see the ruins of Taradell Castle on the nearby hill. From the flagpole walk back towards the trig point and just before reaching it take the path on the left winding downhill. Descend on the winding path and soon the flagpole is above you on your left.

When you reach a well-trodden path, go right downhill. There you rejoin the PR-C 42 route for a while and you can spot the yellow/white signs again. At the junction go right and a few minutes later reach a tarmac road at **Collada de Mansa**. Cross the road and take the path marked 'Castell de Taradell'. (The path on the left is the GR 2 to Aiguafreda.) At the track junction with an information board go left, on the path marked with yellow/white signs. Ignore any paths and stay on the well-trodden path often among dense shrubs. About 15min later arrive at a junction with signposts, surrounded by huge rocks. Go right to **Castell de Taradell** (Castell de can Boix). The remains of the castle on the eroded rocks come into view. It is easy to see why it was a great position for a watchtower as you admire the 360-degree panorama from the ruins. There are some fantastic views of Taradell and to l'Enclusa and beyond.

The **castle** was first mentioned in AD893 in the cartulary of the Cathedral of Vic. It was a watchtower with a purpose of defence but when the Torre de la Plaça was built in 1550 in Taradell, it lost its strategic position. In the 16th century it was listed as a farmhouse and then it was abandoned from the 17th century.

From the ruins take the path by the stone with a memorial plaque. It is a steep, narrow path. At the

junction go right downhill on the steep stony path. Shortly after, when the path is level, notice a wire fence on your left. Descend through forest. Pass by an iron gate as the path bends right downhill. Cross a stream and reach a track about 20min from the castle and go left. Cross the stream again, and continue alongside a fence.

Pass a barrier and at the junction go right downhill. On reaching the tarmac road (B-520) go left and follow the road for a few minutes back to Taradell and retrace your steps to the starting point by **Sant Genis church**.

Castell de Taradell on heavily eroded rocks

WALK 12
Tavèrnoles to Sant Pere de Casserres

Start	Tavèrnoles, car park near the cemetery, N41.953973, E2.327005
Alternative start	Savassona i Sant Feliuet car park, N41.956121, E2.339753
Finish	Sant Pere de Casserres
Distance	11km/8km
Total ascent	390m/290m
Total descent	480m/440m
Grade	2
Time	3hr 30min–4hr or 3hr–3hr 30min
Refreshments	Tavèrnoles has a restaurant/bar on the corner opposite a small playground with a tap. Restaurant in Fucimanya. Restaurant in Sant Pere de Casserres.
Access	Tavèrnoles and Savassona i Sant Feliuet car park are both located on the BV-5213 road near Vic.

This signposted trail offers some fine views and takes you to the Sant Pere de Casserres monastery, overlooking a stunning bend in the river Ter. It is a linear walk but if you want to retrace your steps you can start from Savassona i Sant Feliuet car park and the distance will be more acceptable. Allow plenty of time to explore Savassona i Sant Feliuet and the engraved rocks en route. Also allow at least about 1hr to visit the monastery.

There are plenty of places to park near the cemetery entrance in Tavèrnoles. Follow the yellow/white PR-C 40 signs downhill on Carrer de l'Església. At the junction with a bar/restaurant, cross the main road by the signpost and continue downhill on its other side. Leave that road to the right towards Monastir de Sant Pere de Casserres. You can see many different signs as the GR 151 (Oliba Trail), the PR-C 40 and the GR 210 share this section. When the path splits go right. Shortly after go through a

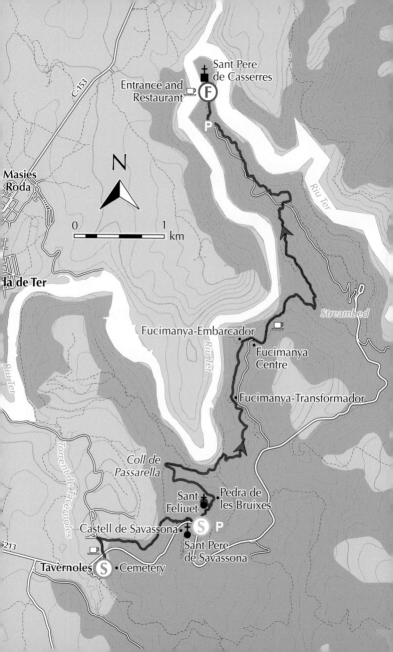

N

0   1 km

Masies Roda

la de Ter

C·153

Sant Pere de Casserres

Entrance and Restaurant

F

P

Riu Ter

Streambed

Fucimanya-Embarcador

Fucimanya Centre

Riu Ter

Fucimanya-Transformador

Riu Ter

Torrent de Tavernoles

Coll de Passarella

Sant Feliuet

Pedra de les Bruixes

Castell de Savassona

S

P

Sant Pere de Savassona

Tavèrnoles   S   Cemetery

213

gate and cross a farmyard. Leave the farmyard through another gate and continue on the path. At the junction with signposts go right towards Monastir de Sant Pere de Casserres uphill on a rocky path that soon gets close to the road (BV-5213). At another junction with a signpost continue straight on (there are both red/white GR 151 and yellow/white PR-C 40 signs marking the route). Ignore any unmarked paths and follow the track.

About 30min from Tavèrnoles, at the junction, go left towards Sant Feliuet (and to Sant Pere de Casserres). Shortly after, the hermitage and a flagpole on the rocky hill come into view. Stay on the well-trodden path ignoring a path on the left. The area is scattered with huge boulders. Arrive at a junction with a signpost. The route to the monastery continues to the right but first go left to make a short detour to Pedra del Sacrifici and then climb the small hill to the hermitage of **Sant Feliuet** (de Savassona). From the summit enjoy the first glimpse of the impressive river Ter. You can also see the buildings of Castell de Savassona on the other side of the main road. ◀

According to legend Pedra del Sacrifici was used for human sacrifices, hence the name, and it is believed that the groove visible on the rock was made by blood.

First documented in AD1035, the sanctuary of **Sant Feliuet de Savassona** was built in the 10th century and then the nave was rebuilt in the 11th century. The hermitage was built on rocks in the centre of a partially excavated ancient Iberian settlement, surrounded by tombs and a cistern carved into rocks. It was restored in 1962 by the Vic Hiking Centre.

As you continue on the path towards the monastery (Monastir Sant Pere), pass some interesting carved rocks along the path: Pedra de l'Home and **Pedra de les Bruixes**.

Under the huge sandstone boulder, **Pedra de la Dau**, some grain storage silos were found. The smaller sandstone boulders, the fascinating Pedra de l'Home and Pedra de les Bruixes, are covered in engravings of crosses, horseshoes and other symbols. Legend has it that the markings on the boulders were made by witches who were in love with the Baron of

Savassona. The markings were meant to be a warning to him as he was part of the Inquisition.

This section of the trail is marked with yellow/white PR-C signs. As you descend through forest you can sometimes glimpse the river. Ignoring a track on the left continue straight on. Also carry straight on by a signpost and cross a wire barrier. Descend through forest and at a junction go right towards the monastery. Turn left onto a path marked with signs for GR 151 Monastir 6.3km, PR-C 40, and GR 210. Pass a wire barrier. There are some views of the river on your left. Look out for the red/white and the yellow/white stripes on trees. Go left downhill at the junction with signs and shortly after, at the next junction, the route goes right downhill. Cross a rocky streambed and then follow the narrow path, first with some views and then among shrubs and trees.

About 45min after leaving the carved rocks, arrive on a dirt track by a transformer building (**Fucimanya-Transformador**) and go left. At the track junction carry straight on. Arrive at Fucimanya Sud (junction) and go right downhill alongside a fence. Ignoring a track on the left continue straight on the grassy path by the fence. Also ignore a track on the left and head towards the houses slightly to the right. Arrive on a tarmac road 15min from the transformer building and go right uphill passing some houses. Reach another tarmac road by the signpost (**Fucimanya Centre**) and go left. At the road junction, go left and pass a playground and some houses. (Go right to visit a restaurant.) At the next junction (Fucimanya Nord), go left downhill.

At the end of the tarmac road go left downhill on a path. Descend on the narrow path and cross a rocky streambed. On reaching a track go left and shortly after, ignoring a track on the left, carry straight on. At the end of the track go uphill on a forest path marked with a yellow/white sign. As you zigzag steeply uphill, look out for the painted waymarkers on the rocks. Reach and cross a tarmac road – the path continues on its other side. Shortly after go left at the junction with clear directional signs.

Junction with clear directional signs

Follow this path with some views of the river for about 30min to reach the monastery's car park, then walk to the monastery, **Sant Pere de Casserres**. You can buy an entrance ticket in the restaurant building. The monastery is a few hundred metres away.

SANT PERE DE CASSERRES

The monastery of Sant Pere de Casserres is a Benedictine monastery built in Romanesque style in the 11th century.

According to legend, the three-day-old son of the Viscount of Osona declared that he wouldn't live for more than 30 days. He suggested that after his death, a mule should be released unguided with his body and where the mule stopped a monastery should be built. The more realistic story of choosing the location of the monastery states that the monastery was built on a site where previously a castle dated back to AD898. The castle had a chapel dedicated to St Peter that the Viscount decided to convert into a monastery.

Viscountess Ermetruit got the work started in 1006 and in 1015 a small community was formed. The basilica we see today was built and consecrated in 1050. In 1079, losing its independence, the monastery was united with the monastery of Cluny. The monastery went into decline between the 13th and 15th centuries. In the 19th century it was in private hands and was used as a farm and tenant house. The Romanesque church has three naves, separated by pillars. The interior was completely decorated with mural paintings but only a few remain.

There is a permanent exhibition of the life of the monks in Casserres in the monastery. For opening times, see www.santperedecasserres.cat.

WALK 13

Puig del Far

Start/finish	Vilanova de Sau, Plaça Major, N41.948072, E2.386658
Distance	8km
Total ascent/descent	350m
Grade	1
Time	3hr
Refreshments	Water fountain at the playground near Santa Maria church. Small restaurant in Vilanova de Sau. None along the way.
Access	Vilanova de Sau is located on the N-141d road which can be accessed from the C-25 road.

From the quiet village of Vilanova de Sau follow the meandering SL-C 122 route to the ruins of a Romanesque church hidden in dense forest. From the summit of Puig del Far – which used to be the location of a signalling tower – enjoy the breathtaking views towards the reservoir, created in 1962. When the water level is low you can see the tower of the submerged church of Sant Romà.

With Santa Maria church behind you, walk along Plaça Mayor and as it splits go right. You can spot red/white GR and green/white SL-C signs. Pass a local trail information board then at the road junction go right on a red/white signed path. Shortly after reach and cross N-141d road and continue on its other side. At the junction go left through a gate. When the path splits go right (this section is marked with GR 151, GR 2, as well as SL-C 122 signs).

Follow the well-trodden forest path marked with both GR and SLC signs, ignoring a path first on the left and shortly after on the right. The path has deep channels in places, carved by rainwater. Zigzag uphill on the rocky path and soon you can take a look back towards Vilanova

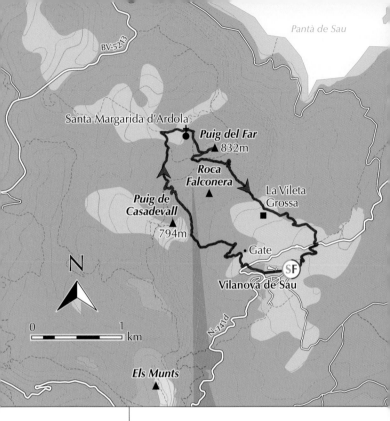

de Sau and you can even make out the distinctive Les
Agudes in the distance.

When the path splits go left on the path marked with
a red/white sign on a rock. A few minutes later, arrive at
a junction with a signpost and take either the track or
the path on the right (as they run parallel). Shortly after,
from either option, reach another track and go left. There
are fenced areas on both sides of the track. Follow the
green/white SL-C signs downhill alongside pastures. (The
GR 151 route leaves the SL-C 122.) Reach a track junction and turn right towards Ermita de Santa Margarida
d'Ardola. Cross a grazing land (take care here as there
might be grazing cows).

The track splits upon reaching the woods. Take the right branch going slightly uphill and shortly after ignore a path on the right. Look out for the ruins of **Santa Margarida d'Ardola** on the right-hand side.

The remains of this **Romanesque church** date back to the 11th century. It was abandoned in 1936 and about a decade later the vaulted ceiling collapsed. Unfortunately not much of it remains today; only two sides of the church wall are still standing. The name 'Ardola' – Iberian in origin – possibly refers to a settlement that might have been located near Puig del Far.

Continue straight on and then go right towards Puig del Far. When the path splits take the left branch uphill. The forest is scattered with huge boulders and rocks. Walk alongside a rock face (there are rock climbing routes here). The path splits; you will continue to Vilanova de Sau downhill to the right, but first take the path on the left. Climb up to the rocky summit of **Puig del Far** (832m), marked with a flagpole. Enjoy the extensive views towards the reservoir encircled by the sheer cliffs of Tavertet.

Extensive views towards the reservoir surrounded by the sheer cliffs of Tavertet

You might spot the submerged church tower in the reservoir if water levels are low and could even see the silhouettes of the highest peaks of the Montseny Natural Park. ◄

From the summit retrace your steps to the way-marked junction and go left downhill towards Vilanova de Sau. Ignore any unmarked paths on either side of the main well-trodden path and reach a small waterhole – used by wildlife – and go left on the marked path. About 50 metres later go left on the SL-C 122 trail downhill and a few minutes later reach a dirt track and go left. Follow it for about 50 metres and then leave it to the right on the green/white marked path. Go through a narrow wooden barrier (designed to keep bikers out) and descend on a rocky path. There are some views towards Vilanova de Sau. Zigzag downhill following the signs and ignoring any other paths.

Arrive on a narrow tarmac road by a farm building (**La Vileta Grossa**) and go left. There are views towards the rocky cliffs on your left. Follow the tarmac road alongside grazing fields and some houses until you reach the N-141d road. Go left and after a short distance go right by the signpost towards Vilanova de Sau. Ignore a path on the right-hand side of the road and continue towards Vilanova de Sau. Ignore a track on the left as you follow the tarmac, and shortly spot the church tower. About an hour after leaving Puig del Far arrive back at **Santa Maria church** on Plaça Major.

WALK 14

Vilanova de Sau to Pont de Malafogassa

Start/finish	Vilanova de Sau, Plaça Major, N41.948072, E2.386658
Distance	7km (there and back)
Total ascent/descent	190m
Grade	1
Time	2hr–2hr 30min
Refreshments	Water fountain at the playground next to the church and snack bar/restaurant in Vilanova de Sau. Water at the campsite near Pont de Malafogassa.
Access	Vilanova de Sau is located on the N-141d road which can be accessed from the C-25 road.

This is a short, delightful there-and-back route through woodland to a Gothic stone bridge. The Riera Major riverbank near the bridge is a great spot for a picnic. The trail described is the waymarked SL-C 121 trail and is easy to follow.

Facing Santa Maria church go right downhill on the tarmac road. At the junction turn right towards Pont de Malafogassa (you can see the green/white SL-C 121 sign). Descend on the tarmac road and at a bend in the road cross over a bridge. After about 10min from the church, reach a junction by a house. Continue straight on and after 50 metres go left on the track marked SL-C 121 just after the house. Walk past a grazing field and then the track narrows down to a path and goes alongside a wall. Shortly after cross a streambed over a bridge and then ascend through forest.

Follow the green/white signs on the well-trodden path for about 15min ignoring any other paths and reach a tarmac road. Cross it, then the marked trail continues on the other side. Follow the SL-C 121 signs ignoring any side paths for about 10–15min and when the track

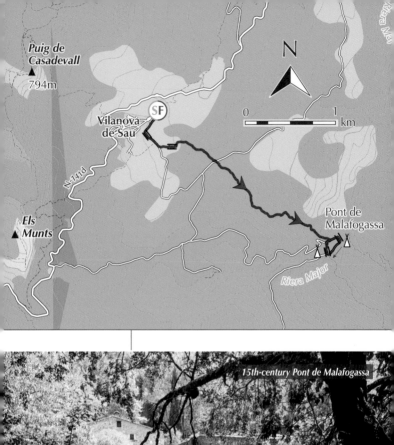

Puig de
Casadevall
▲
794m

Vilanova
de Sau

SF

N

0   1
km

N-141d

Els
▲ Munts

Pont de
Malafogassa

Riera Major

15th-century Pont de Malafogassa

splits (no signs here), go left uphill. Shortly after descend through forest with some views on your right for a further 15min and arrive at a junction with a signpost.

Cross the bridge over Riera Major

There is a sign to Pont de Malafogassa both ways: you will make a small loop. First go left and reach the 15th-century bridge (**Pont de Malafogassa**). Cross over and go right, passing a campsite building. Continue through the camping ground and when you reach a tarmac road go right. Cross the bridge over Riera Major and pass the main entrance of the **campsite** (Camping El Pont). Keep right and reach the junction with the signpost to close the loop. Go left and retrace your steps to **Vilanova de Sau**.

> **Pont de Malafogassa** was built in 1498 on the ruins of an earlier bridge that was destroyed by an earthquake between 1425 and 1427. It was financed by the residents of Vilanova de Sau, Bancells, Querós and Castanyedell. The Gothic stone bridge stretches over Riera Major with two voussoir arches supported by three pillars.

WALK 15
Tavertet circular

Start/finish	Tavertet town hall/Information Centre, N41.996942, E2.418751
Distance	11km
Total ascent/descent	880m
Grade	3
Time	4hr 30min–5hr
Refreshments	Restaurants and cafés at Tavertet. Snack bar by Mirador de Castell.
Access	BV-5207 road. There is a car park for visitors outside of the village. It costs €2 for a day but you will need coins for the machine when leaving the car park.

Enjoy some incredible views towards a reservoir with the partially submerged Sant Romà church, as well as of Puig del Far above Vilanova de Sau. The trail described follows a wide track on top of the cliffs of Tavertet before heading to Puig de la Força. The route then takes some lesser-used paths which are very steep and narrow so sure-footedness is required. The return leg follows a section of the GR 2 long-distance trail.

Walk into the village where there is an information board about local walks. Continue straight on past a restaurant and a wash house and keep right. Pass the church on the main square, and shortly after pass the Mirador de Tavertet (viewpoint). Then take the dirt track on the left. Pass some signs and by the information board notice the narrow trail marked with GR 2 going steeply downhill on the left-hand side of the track. You will return on this path.

Follow the wide track towards Puig de la Força, ignoring any unmarked side paths. However, look out for the marked MTB track on the left-hand side, opposite the 'La Cantina de Virupa 0.8km' signpost. Follow this

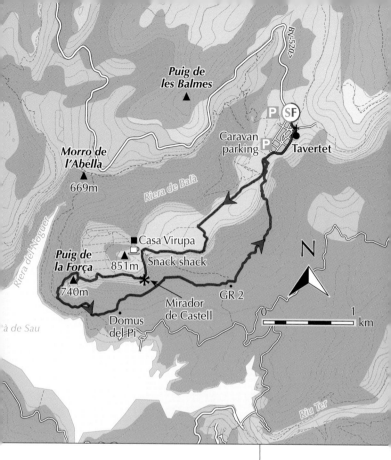

bike track which takes you closer to the edge of the cliffs with impressive views of the mountains, sheer rock walls and the reservoir on your left. Arrive back on the track (that you left earlier) near a building. Go left and pass **La Cantina snack shack**. Ignore a track heading to Casa Virupa health retreat. Continue on the track and about 45min after leaving Tavertet arrive at **Mirador de Castell**. From there you can enjoy some fantastic views of the reservoir and the mountains, all the way to the Montseny mountains in the distance.

SAU RESERVOIR

The dam was built on the Ter River, creating a reservoir near the village of Vilanova de Sau in 1962. The water covered the former village of Sant Romà de Sau and the tower of Sant Romà church is visible when the water level is low. People can hire a kayak and paddle around the partially submerged church tower.

From Mirador de Castell continue on the track for about 200 metres and then look out for a rock cairn on the left-hand side of the track. This marks the way to Puig de la Força, but there are no other signs. Take the narrow path steeply downhill keeping slightly right with views of the reservoir on your left. Look out for some faint red marks painted on the rocks. Soon descend on old, steep stone steps. The steps are in poor condition so take extra care. Reach a more obvious path on the ledge and go right by the rock wall. Walk beneath eroded overhanging rocks (*balma* in Catalan) and then onto the ledge. Puig de la Força is towering in front of you.

When you think that you have reached the end of the path, as you get close to the drop, notice the remains of a stone wall across the drop. Just below the rock you are

Walk beneath eroded overhanging rocks

standing on there are some steps. Go down the steps and then along a narrow ridge through woods. Shortly after notice an information sign and a path going downhill to the right. You will follow that path steeply downhill, but first continue straight on. Climb steeply, sometimes on rocks, and a few minutes later reach the summit of **Puig de la Força**, 740m. Enjoy some spectacular views of the reservoir and the magnificent cliffs.

Spectacular views of the reservoir

> There was a castle on this mountain but today only a small part of a tower and wall remains. **Castell del Puig de la Força**, otherwise known as Castell Cornil, was probably built around the 10th century and first documented in 917.

Retrace your steps to the sign and then take the narrow, steep path (now on your left) downhill. This is a very steep section that can be slippery and loose in places. Descend among shrubs and trees for about 15min and then walk alongside a rock face on your left. Look out for rock cairns marking the path. Notice the track below and shortly arrive on the track and go left. Follow the track on the mountainside with views of the reservoir on your right. Go through a chain barrier and continue downhill. There are some fascinating red and grey cliffs towering above on your left. Cross a wire barrier and walk through woods scattered with boulders. At a track junction look out for the green/white SL-C 94 and the red/white GR signs and follow these on a path to the left. At the next junction carry straight on towards Domus del Pi and Places Carboneres. A few minutes later at a junction, the SL-C94 route continues to the left towards 'Places Carboneres', but first take a detour to **Domus del Pi** to the right. After the detour to the historical building, continue on the SL-C 94 towards Places Carboneres.

> The **Domus del Pi**, first documented in the 11th century, was a fortified building complete with walls and a moat. The existing part of the building was probably the lower floor of a tower. It was built in Romanesque style with a barrel vaulted ceiling. It exchanged hands quite a few times over the centuries, but it is almost certain that it was continuously occupied until the 19th century.

Shortly turn right on the SL-C 94 marked narrow trail going uphill. Reach an information board and the first of several charcoal burning places (*plaça carbonera*). Continue on the narrow path with some views towards the reservoir, passing further charcoal burning places. When the path widens in a junction continue straight on, on the path marked with red/white GR 2 and GR 151 signs, leaving the SL-C 94 trail as it goes to the right.

Go through a wire livestock barrier and at a junction, go left towards Tavertet. Ignore the track on the left and as you ascend look out for GR 2 signs. Reach and cross a dirt track and continue on its other side. This is a steep ascent. Look out for the red/white GR signs as you zigzag uphill. Soon you have some amazing views of the cliffs below Tavertet and you can spot the Mirador de Tavertet (viewpoint) above in the village. Walk alongside the cliff and then zigzag uphill. Arrive on a dirt track and turn right and walk back to **Tavertet**.

SANT LLORENÇ DEL MUNT I L'OBAC NATURAL PARK

You can make a short detour to Morral del Drac on Walk 19

Monestir de Sant Llorenç del Munt (Walk 19)

SANT LLORENÇ DEL MUNT I L'OBAC NATURAL PARK

This natural park offers a great number of trails among fascinating rock formations and on slopes covered by oak woodlands. Several routes lead to the summits of Montcau and La Mola with a monastery building and a small restaurant to welcome hikers. The long-distance trail, the Els 3 Monts which connects the three mountain ranges (Montseny, Sant Llorenç and Montserrat), traverses through the natural park. Follow a section of this trail to Mura (Walk 21) and then spend some time wandering its centuries-old narrow streets. Find a welcoming café or restaurant and soak in the atmosphere. You can base yourself near the natural park; Matadepera, Sabadell or Terrassa are the bigger towns that cater for walkers in the area. The hot springs found in Caldes de Montbui have been used since Roman times. Not surprisingly there is a Roman bath and other Roman buildings in this small town. The water emerges at 74°C from the Lion's fountain on the main square and the spa hotels entice people to stay in town for longer than an afternoon.

There are regular trains from Terrassa and Sabadell. The TGO bus company operate local buses: https://www.gruptg.com/.

WALK 16
Sant Miquel del Fai circular

Start/finish	Sant Miquel del Fai car park, N41.716117, E2.191639
Distance	7km
Total ascent/descent	610m
Grade	1
Time	2hr 30min
Refreshments	None
Access	Sant Miquel del Fai car park is located 7km north of Sant Feliu de Codines, along the BV-1485 road.

Sant Miquel del Fai is a monastery overlooking a deep river gorge that was formed by two rivers, the Tenes and Rossinyol. This short walk enables you to admire the impressive cliffs of Bertí, the Tenes river valley and some waterfalls below the monastery building and across the valley. At the time of writing the monastery is closed for restoration.

With the stone bridge on your right follow the tarmac road, and a few metres later leave the road to the right on the GR 5 path marked red/white. Cross a streambed and then keep right on the path marked with a red/white GR sign. Ascend on a narrow path marked with red/white GR signs. A path on the right leads to a rocky outcrop – an ideal vantage point to admire the monastery and its dramatic surroundings from. Across the valley, the BV-1485 is clearly visible cut into the mountainside. Ignore a path with a red/white 'X' on the right and shortly after the waymarked path bends away from the gorge. Pass some ruins and then the village of Riells del Fai comes into view, down below on the right.

The path then levels and runs along the mountainside among shrubs. The landscape is dominated by fascinating red cliffs. Reach a junction marked only with a rock cairn (about 3km from your start point) and go right, leaving the GR 5 trail.

For further views you can take a short detour to a nearby outcrop marked with a flagpole (**Turó de l'Ullar**, 648m). For the viewpoint follow the GR signs for a further 50 metres and then look out for a narrow, overgrown path on the right which will lead you to the viewpoint. Enjoy some views towards Riells del Fai and the dramatic cliffs before retracing your steps to the junction with the rock cairn, then go left downhill leaving the GR 5 trail.

Descend steeply on a rocky path. The path then levels for a while as you walk along the foot of a rock face

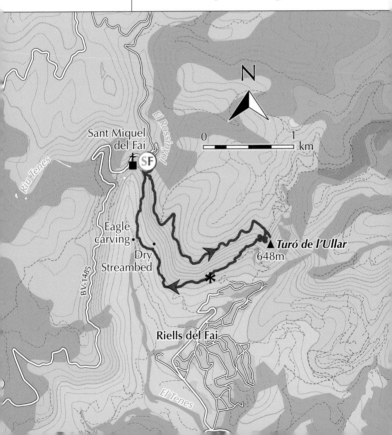

on your right. Turn sharply left downhill at a sizeable rock. Zigzag steeply downhill. When you reach another path go right, more or less parallel to the cliffs above on your right. Follow the path along the ledge and notice a drystone wall on your right. Go left steeply downhill on a path marked with cairns, initially on a flat piece of rock. Descend on the path marked by rock cairns towards the village. Reach another path and go right. Shortly pass a rocky outcrop with a flagpole, providing an excellent **viewpoint** towards Riells del Fai. The path gets closer to the reddish rock cliffs and then turns towards the river valley in the direction of Sant Miquel del Fai.

Stay close to the cliffs as you walk away from the village and spot some houses down below in the valley. Soon cross a dry streambed and then arrive at a junction with a signpost and an eagle carving made of wood. Go right towards Sant Miquel del Fai. Follow this path with views of the valley. Notice some ruins of industrial buildings in the valley and on the opposite side. After an uphill section reach a signpost by cliffs and continue towards the monastery and subsequently back through

The rocky outcrop is an ideal vantage point from which to admire the monastery

The path goes more or less parallel to the cliffs above the village

a narrow gap in the rocks and to the car park at **Sant Miquel del Fai**.

The area of **Sant Miquel del Fai** has been a place of worship for many centuries. The first documentation dates back to 887. At first there was only a Romanesque shrine and the church of Sant Miquel here and then the land was acquired by a nobleman, Gombau de Besora, who founded the monastery in the late 10th century. The priory itself was only built in the 15th century. A narrow path runs along the ledge to the ruins of a hermitage which was the original church.

WALK 17

Montcau and Cova Simanya

Start/finish	Marquet de les Roques car park at the cultural centre, N41.676678, E2.020899
Distance	9km
Total ascent/descent	650m
Grade	3 (some route-finding difficulties)
Time	4hr
Refreshments	Font de Llor but take ample water for the day.
Access	From the B-124 road, approximately 2km south of San Llorenc Savall, take the road towards Val d'Horta and follow it for about 3km to Marquet de les Roques.

This lesser-known route gives plenty of opportunities to marvel at the fascinating rock formations of Sant Llorenç Natural Park. It then joins the well-trodden path that leads to the summit of Montcau. There is an option to make a detour to Cova Simanya (Simanya Cave) and other caves – however, at the time of writing this was closed to the public (see notes below). The scenery is dominated by rounded rocks and far-reaching views.

MARQUET DE LES ROQUES

The Neo-Romanesque building was built in the late 19th century on the ruins of a 13th-century farmhouse. It was the Catalan poet Joan Oliver's (1899–1986) summer house where he organized literary gatherings and exhibitions. Today the building houses an information point for the natural park and also serves as a cultural centre.

The Neo-Romanesque building of Marquet de les Roques

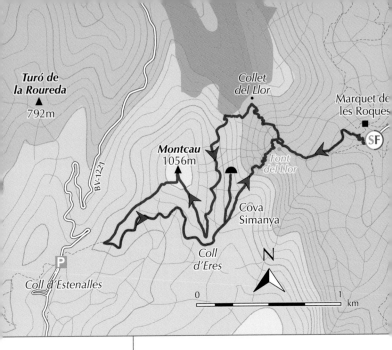

Note: map scale
is 1:25,000

From the map board go right towards Font del Llor, down-hill. Cross over the bridge, go left and then head to the building, **Marquet de les Roques**. Turn left here (there are signs for the GR 5 and the Els 3 Monts IP-4, as this first part of the trail is also part of those long-distance trails).

At the junction by a small building (Pont de la Font del Llor) go right uphill on the path marked with a GR 5 sign, towards Font del Llor. Shortly after (1km from the start) at the steps leading to the spring (**Font del Llor**) go right uphill on the GR 5 path. You will return from the direction of Font del Llor. Every so often the trees give way to views of towering rocks as you zigzag steeply uphill. When you reach a flat area (**Collet del Llor**) go left (Els Emprius is marked to the right).

Ignore a faint path on the right shortly after the junction. Follow the narrow path uphill among trees and shrubs. At the junction on a clearing the GR 5 path goes left, but take the second path (unmarked and faint) on the right through bushes. This is a steep uphill section among shrubs and oaks; look out for the path as it might not always be obvious. Before long, walk on solid rock and you can see the building of Marquet de les Roques and the car park down below.

Follow the path along the ledge and then keep uphill as the path bends right. The path might be less obvious here but as you climb uphill on this steep rocky terrain look out for rock cairns. Join a more prominent path and keep left. ▶ Shortly after follow the ledge with views of the rocky landscape. Traverse a steep section sloping sideways and shortly after reach a well-trodden path. Go right and climb for about 10–15min to reach the peak of **Montcau**, 1056m. The ridge leads the eye all the way to La Mola and the 360-degree panorama is dominated by the mountains of the Sant Llorenç del Munt I l'Obac Natural Park.

From the summit descend back a little to the path where there are few steps and go right downhill (heading west-south-west). Descend – steeply at times – with Montcau behind you for about 15min, then reach a track and go left. (This is part of the popular shorter route to

The path is fringed by low shrubs.

The well-trodden path to the top of Montcau

Montcau from Coll d'Estenalles. Its car park is 400 metres down to the right.) Follow the track skirting around Montcau for about 10–15min and reach Coll d'Eres where several paths converge. Continue towards Cova Simanya on the GR 5 path downhill. Descend through forest and a few minutes later at a path junction (which you will return to) go left to the caves at **Cova Simanya**.

> Due to archaeological excavation **Cova Simanya** is closed to the public. However, for a small fee you can join a guided tour if you want to visit the cave. Guided tours start from Coll d'Estenalles and must be pre-booked. For the latest information check https://parcs.diba.cat

Arriving back at the junction from the caves, continue left and downhill towards Font del Llor on a narrow path south-west. When the path splits by a huge boulder, leave the GR 5 trail and continue straight on steeply downhill (the GR 5 takes a slightly longer route to the Font del Llor). The path runs alongside a streambed on your left. Ignore a path on the right and continue downhill close to the streambed. As you zigzag steeply downhill, occasionally the trees give way to views of rocky mountainsides. Stay on the right side of the riverbed (there is a huge boulder in the middle) and make your way downhill between boulders. Notice the railings near the spring. Arrive at Font del Llor about 30min after leaving the GR 5 trail. Keep left when you reach the spring and a few metres later arrive back at the steps where you took the GR 5 uphill earlier. Continue straight on and retrace your steps back to the car park at **Marquet de les Roques**.

WALK 18
Castellasa circular

Start/finish	Matadepera, Masia la Tartana, N41.610671, E2.032012
Distance	8.5km
Total ascent/descent	500m
Grade	2
Time	3hr–3hr 30min
Refreshments	Available in Matadepera. None along the way.
Access	The walk starts at the end of Carrer de Camí de la Font de la Tartana/Camí de Can Torres just after the main gate of Masia la Tartana in Matadepera.

This lovely route is less popular than other trails in the area but treats you to some amazing views of interesting rock formations. The trail is partially waymarked and makes use of tracks and narrow paths. There is also a short section where sure-footedness might be required.

You can park along Carrer del Camí de la Font de la Tartana. There is a signpost (Can Solà del Racó) at the end of the road where the road splits. Go left steeply uphill (you will return via the other track). This first section of the trail is part of the PR-C 31 and GR 173 routes. The steep tarmac road becomes a dirt track. At a junction go right. Shortly after notice the remains of an old **kiln** by the left-hand side of the track. ▶

There are some views of tree-covered mountains.

The track becomes surfaced and at a major junction (**Collet de Pujol**), by a red fire hydrant, go right on the path marked with a red/white 'X'. Head slightly left uphill. Skirt around the left side of a rocky top and then follow the ridge populated with pines and oaks. La Mola comes into view in the distance. Follow the undulating ridge, ignoring a path going downhill on the left. Join a track and continue straight on uphill towards the

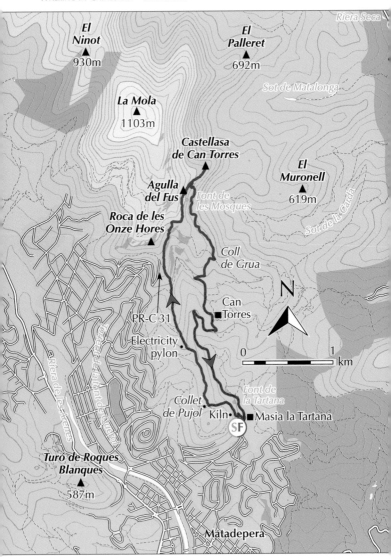

electricity pylon. Pass the pylon and, shortly after, the track becomes surfaced.

Take care as you follow the rocky ledge

About 100 metres past the electricity pylon look out for a narrow path on the right. Take this path, initially running parallel to the track. When it splits take the left branch uphill and immediately after ignore a path crossing. On reaching a dirt track go right, slightly uphill. Ignore a track joining from the left and 50 metres later carry straight on uphill. Ignore any side paths and on reaching a fence carry straight on, briefly joining the PR-C 31 route (to La Mola) marked with yellow/white signs. Shortly after reach a map board, just under an hour from the start. Leaving the marked trail, take the narrow path on the right with the map board on your left. Follow this path on the mountainside among shrubs for a few minutes and just before reaching a streambed (Sot de la Sodoleda), go left uphill on the path. The trail

Impressive rock formation of Castellasa de Can Torres

might not be waymarked here but follow the distinguishable path uphill.

Ignore a path going steeply downhill on the right and shortly after reach a well-trodden path. Bear right and then immediately left. Follow the contour of the mountainside with some amazing views of the mountains in the distance as well as the nearby cliffs, and you can also see the rock formation, Castellasa de Can Torres. Take care as you follow the rocky ledge by the cliffs as it can be slippery.

Then walk through a wooded area, ignoring a path on the left heading towards a rock wall. Descend a little and then traverse by cliffs again. The path can be slippery in places. Ignore a path going steeply downhill on the right (you will take this path when returning from Castellasa de Can Torres). As you carry straight on, notice some blue and yellow marks painted on the rocks. Ignore a path on the left turning towards rocks and continue on the ledge and then among trees. Reach **Castellasa de Can Torres**, a fascinating rock formation, about 40min from the map board.

The formation of the monolith in the Sant Llorenç del Munt massif began some 55 million years ago. The area used to be the shoreline of an ancient inland sea. When the sea disappeared, as a result of tectonic movements, the delta created by a river rose and made the first formation of the Sant Llorenç del Munt massif. **Castellasa de Can Torres** was originally attached to the massif. However, fractures, erosion and landslides isolated the monolith from the cliff.

From Castellasa, retrace your steps back to the first path on the left. Go steeply downhill and shortly notice some painted white/grey marks on rocks. Descend among bushes. As you zigzag downhill you might also notice some blue and yellow paint marks. Occasionally views open up towards the mountains. At a rocky clearing join another path and keep right. Follow the rocky ledge, pass **Font de les Mosques** (no more than drips from a rock) and shortly after walk through woods again. If you look back, you can make out Castellasa. Follow the undulating path through the forest.

About 30min from Castellasa arrive at a dirt track and go left downhill. Follow the track for 50 metres and then take the narrow path on the right (**Coll de Grua**). At a junction go right downhill on a track and a few minutes later arrive on a dirt track. Go left here. Ignore a track joining from the left and continue straight on downhill. When the track splits take the right fork towards a building (**Can Torres**). After the house carry straight on by the signs. Ignore any paths and follow this track downhill. The dirt track becomes a surfaced road, and then a dirt track again. About 20min from Can Torres, keep right by the next signpost with the riverbed on your left. Shortly after walk alongside a fence, passing a picnic area with a spring (**Font de la Tartana**). Pass some houses and arrive back at your starting point on the outskirts of **Matadepera**.

WALK 19
La Mola from Torre de l'Àngel

Start/finish	Torre de l'Àngel car park, Matadepera, N41.627464, E1.999043
Distance	10.5km
Total ascent/descent	570m
Grade	2
Time	3hr 30min
Refreshments	Restaurant in the monastery building on La Mola.
Access	Torre de l'Àngel car park is located on the BV-1221 road, just outside of Matadepera.

Many trails lead to the monastery on La Mola, the highest peak in the St Llorenç del Munt i l'Obac Natural Park. While most walkers take the well-trodden path from Matadepera, this circular route (on the SL-C 50 trail) is a great alternative, offering some really spectacular views on the way. The first part of the trail is occasionally steep and it can take nearly two hours to reach the summit.

Follow the dirt track from the car park, passing a modernist-style building on your left. Ignoring a path on the right, continue in a dry riverbed. A few minutes later go right on the forest track marked with a green/white SL-C 50 trail sign. Follow the forest track and at the junction go right towards Can Robert/La Mola. Pass the remains of a lime kiln and at the junction turn left. A few minutes later arrive at **Can Robert car park**. (Confusingly the SL-C trail signs mark two paths from the car park but they rejoin after the small reservoir.) From Can Robert car park follow the path starting by the information board. Climb uphill through forest with a small reservoir on your left. Arrive on a path by a stone building and turn left uphill. Shortly after keep right on the marked trail. Ascend on the rocky path passing the **Tombes de Can Robert**.

Tombes de Can Robert, the **medieval necropolis**, dates back to the seventh–ninth centuries, the transition period between Roman and medieval times. Local stones were used for the tombs, positioned in rows in west-east orientation.

At the junction continue straight on uphill on the wide track. The dirt track becomes a surfaced track for a short section. When the SL-C 50 trail splits, go left on the Canal de l'Abella /Morral del Drac route. (You will return to this junction from the track marked 'Can

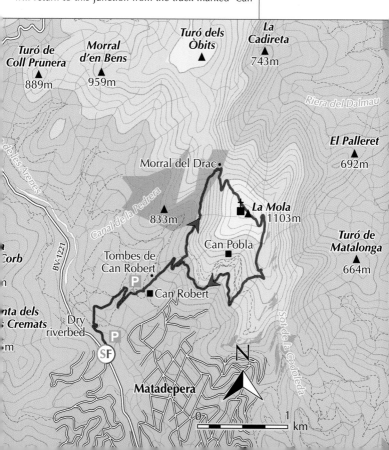

Views open up all the way to the Montserrat range

Pobla la Mola per cami dels Monjos'.) Climb towards the towering rocks, initially on rocks and then on a narrow path among shrubs. Reach a wider path and go left and slightly downhill, with the scenery dominated by towering rocks. On a clear day you can make out the Montserrat range in the distance. Walk through woods, occasionally with a steep drop on the left. Pass the remains of a lime kiln as you climb through the forest towards La Mola. Emerge onto another path and go right towards La Mola.

Here, first make a short detour straight on to **Morral del Drac**, a huge monolith. From there the path to La Mola is also marked with 'Els 3 Monts IP-4' signs. Soon walk with the rock face on your left and on the other side views open up all the way to the Montserrat range.

Follow the green/white signs slightly left uphill on rocks and then through woods surrounded by towering rocks on both sides. A few minutes later at a rocky clearing keep right uphill on the rocks. As you head towards the monastery building you can enjoy some fine views and then from the summit of **La Mola** (1103m) – on a clear day – you can even make out the Pyrenees in the distance. Montcau and the nearby mountains of Sant Llorenç Natural Park dominate the immediate scenery.

> The first record of a **religious community** here dates back to as early as AD986 and there is a mention of an abbot in Sant Llorenç del Munt in 1018. The Romanesque building was built during the 11th century and it was inhabited by Benedictine monks until 1608. However, it started to decline during the 12th century and it was abandoned after 1637. Napoleon's troops destroyed the monastery and the current building was constructed in the late 19th century in a Catalan Romanesque style without altering the original design.

From the viewpoint by the monastery building follow the SL-C 50 signs towards Can Robert, going downhill to a gate. This part of the trail is also marked with PR-C 31 signs. Shortly after ignore a narrow path on the left (to Font del Saüc) and continue downhill. Also ignore the path to Avenc de Cau Pobla on the right.

About 20–25min from the summit, at a junction, go right towards Can Robert. Descend through woods. At the junction continue straight on downhill and spot some yellow arrows on the rock steps. Reach a junction – where you see the PR-C 31 trail sign again – and continue straight on downhill on the SL-C 50 marked trail. Shortly after ignore a path on the right. Also carry straight on at the next junction and reach a wide path. Keep left and then follow the path as it bends right downhill (ignoring any other paths). ▶ Cross a small streambed over a concrete bridge and walk through shrubs.

Emerge onto a track and turn left. Ignore a track on the right and descend on the well-trodden track. This track becomes surfaced for a short section. At the junction (where you originally went up to La Mola) go left downhill and retrace your steps (about 15min) to Can Robert car park, then continue on to **Torre de l'Àngel car park** (about another 10min).

Spot the imposing Can Pobla nestled on the rocky mountainside with towering rocks behind the building.

WALK 20
Alzina del Salari circular

Start/finish	Alzina del Salari car park, N41.653034, E1.977339
Distance	8km
Total ascent/descent	440m
Grade	2 (some route-finding difficulties)
Time	2hr 30min–3hr
Refreshments	Font de la Pola
Access	Alzina del Salari car park is located along the BV-1221 road, about 4km north of Matadepera.

Views towards the jagged Montserrat range accompany you for almost this entire route. Stop for a rest at Font de la Pola, the shaded place with a spring which has been a popular stopping place for hunters and hikers. The trail described is not waymarked and you might want to use GPS to help you navigate this rugged landscape criss-crossed by many paths.

With the information board on your right walk uphill on the tarmac track. At the end of the parking area, at the T-junction, turn left and shortly after at the next junction go right uphill on tarmac. Ignoring a path joining from the right, go left on the tarmac track that shortly becomes a wide trail. Ignore a path on the right and continue on the forest path, and when it splits take the right branch. This follows the contour of the mountainside and soon views open up towards La Mola. A few minutes later when this wide path splits, go right uphill. Ascend the stony path, ignoring a path joining from the left. Reach **Coll de Tres Creus** (a five-way junction) about 20min from Alzina del Salari car park. Continue straight on towards Font de la Pola, crossing the GR 5 trail. Views open up towards the jagged Montserrat range.

Don't let the great views take all your attention; take care as you follow the rocky path on the ledge. Pass a small cove and follow the contour of the mountainside. About 15min from Tres Creus the path splits. Take the right branch, among bushes (you will be returning to this junction and then continuing on the other branch going slightly downhill) and arrive at a huge rock face and **Font de la Pola**.

This shaded place with fresh drinking water was a popular stopping place for hunters and hikers. In 1928 a group of friends (Valentí Rossinyol,

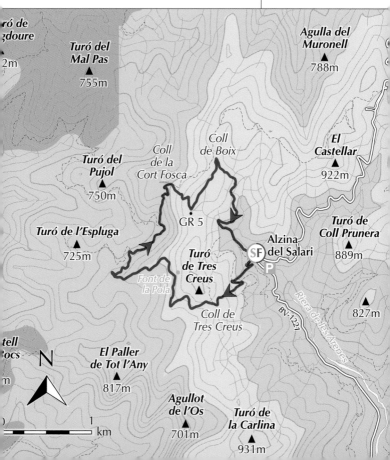

known as El Tinet, Pere Pallejà and Hans Weichsel) started a project to create a **recreation area** here. With help of the Terrassa Youth, a stone basin for water and a round stone table with a chessboard painted on it were built. As soon as the first phase of the construction finished more people started to visit the place. A small pantry was also made by the builders, where they kept pans and cooking utensils. Anyone could ask for the pantry's key to use anything from the pantry, and in return people left a small donation in the piggy bank. This system was in place until the 1950s when the pantry was looted. Rossinyol and his friends visited the spring almost every weekend, and until the Spanish Civil War they spent a whole week there every August.

From the spring, retrace your steps to the split in the trail and take the path on the right. Descend among shrubs. Ignore a path on the right (which would take you back to the spring). Shortly after, as you follow the rocky ledge, views open up towards the serrated Montserrat range. Ignore any faint paths and stay on the well-trodden trail. The path splits twice in quick succession; go left both times through woods and then walk by the cliffs where you can enjoy further views towards Montserrat. Shortly after, walk through a forested area again ignoring a path on the left. You might notice some painted green/white marks on the rocks. Ignore a path on the right and continue downhill through forest. At a clearing go slightly right, marked with a green arrow on a rock. As you descend look out for green signs. At the T-junction, turn right. The path might be overgrown in places.

About 35min from Font de la Pola emerge onto a wider path and go right. Follow the contour of the mountainside, and when the track splits take the right branch uphill. Ascend ignoring the huge stone steps on the right and a few minutes later also ignore a narrow rocky path on the left. At the junction, where a path joins a track, take the second path on the right and climb the 'steps'. The Montserrat range in the distance is visible on your right as you walk through shrubs. Follow the undulating path and when you reach the GR 5 trail go left. Shortly after ignore a path on the left and carry straight on. There are some views towards La Mola. Follow the red/white signs among trees.

Arrive at **Coll de Boix** (a junction) about 10–15min after you joined the GR 5 trail. Turn sharply right downhill (the first path on the right, just before the sign). Descend ignoring a path on the right at a rocky clearing and shortly after also ignore a path on the left. Zigzag downhill on the rocky path. Ignoring a path on the left, continue steeply downhill on the well-trodden path. About 15min from Coll de Boix leave this well-trodden path to the right, going uphill among bushes. At the junction go left downhill on a wider stony path, and shortly after ignore a faint path joining from right. At the next junction continue straight on, on the wide path downhill alongside a rock wall. A few minutes later arrive back at the **car park** by the information board.

WALK 21

Coll d'Estenalles to Mura

Start	Coll d'Estenalles, N41.669796, E1.994658
Finish	Mura
Distance	9km
Total ascent	100m
Total descent	510m
Grade	1
Time	3hr
Refreshments	Cafés and restaurants in Mura. None along the way.
Access	Coll d'Estenalles and its large car park are on the BV-1221 road, about 11km north of Matadepera.

This section of the Els 3 Monts trail takes you to the charming village of Mura, allowing you to admire the characteristic landscape along the way. It is worth spending some time wandering the steep, narrow streets of Mura. At the time of writing there were two buses in the afternoon from Mura to Coll d'Estenalles, but check the timetable locally. However, it is an easy trail and you can retrace your steps to Coll d'Estenalles if you don't want to rely on buses.

The GR 5 trail to Coll de Boix and the Els 3 Monts trail (section IP-4) to Mura start at the end of Coll d'Estenalles car park opposite the information building. Climb the steps and then keep right uphill on a wide path. Spot a large building, La Mata, on the hillside. This 16th-century farmhouse is home to the offices of the Sant Llorenç Natural Park. Follow the path, getting close to a dirt track but turning right uphill away from the track and then going left on the GR 5 trail. Follow the GR 5 signs, pass a small reservoir and go right towards Coll de Boix. Pass a chain barrier. The top of the 16th-century chapel, Ermita de Sant Jaume, is visible on your left. As you descend you might have a glimpse of La Mola. Continue straight on at a junction (with Font Freda 700m to the right).

Puig
Gili
663m
BV-1223

Cantacorbs
675m

F Mura

Sant Martí

Playground

Torrent d'Estenalles

L'Ocell
de Pedra
739m

BV-1221

▲ El Castellot

Torrent de El Reixac

El Cargol

Pujol del Llobet
745m

Cova de
Mura

Junction

Queixa
Corcat
867m

Turó de
la Roureda
792m

Roques de
la Coca
▲

Puigbò
772m

Torrent de Fontfreda

Agulla del
Muronell
788m

Montcau
1056m
▲

Reservoir

S Coll d'Estenalles

P

†

oca del Sot
Mata-rodona
751m

La
Mata

Coll
de Boix

BV-1221

N

Canal de les Teixoneres

Turó de
Coll Prunera
889m

Morral
d'en Bens
959m

Torrent de les Planes

827m

1
km

Ignore the paths marked with a red/white 'X' and a few minutes later at a junction carry straight on. There are some great views of Montcau. Leaving the wide path, go left on the GR 5 path towards Coll de Boix. Shortly after follow the rocky ledge and about 45–50min from Coll d'Estenalles arrive at **Coll de Boix**. Several paths meet here. Go right towards Mura, leaving the GR 5 trail. This section is waymarked with 'Els 3 Monts IP-4' (green/white) signs. Reach a wide path and go right.

Ignore an unmarked path on the left but shortly after leave the wide path to the left by the signpost to Mura, and then go left on the marked path downhill. Descend among trees ignoring another path on the left. Follow the waymarked path ignoring two joining paths from the right. From a rocky ridge enjoy some views towards Montcau as well as of the Monsterrat range. Shortly after descend among trees. When the path splits (about 20min after leaving the wide path) go right downhill; this is only marked with a rock cairn. Descend among trees and shortly after the peak of Montcau comes into view once again. Keep right among shrubs and then continue on the rocky ledge. Follow the rock cairns downhill and about 45min from Coll de Boix reach a **junction** with signs. Join the SL-C 69 route. Take the right branch to enjoy further views of the nearby mountains, but the other branch would also take you to Mura.

Continue straight on towards El Cargol/El Castellot, marked with signs for SL-C 69 as well as Els 3 Monts (IP 4). As you follow the path, enjoy some further views towards Montcau and you may be able to make out the rugged peaks of the Monsterrat mountains in the distance. About 15min from the junction, reach **El Cargol** (a seasonal spring) and continue downhill, first among shrubs and trees and then on a ridge. About 10min after El Cargol pass **El Castellot**, a towering rock formation. Juniper and rosemary populate the hillside by the path. Descend among shrubs. Ignore a path on the left to Mura and stay on the marked path. Pass an electric pylon. The view is dominated by the houses of Mura nestled on the hillside.

Arrive on a surfaced road and go right. There are some allotments by the track. Follow the surfaced road downhill for a few minutes ignoring any paths on either side of the road. Cross a streambed and continue on the Carrer Joan Alavedra track parallel to the road, passing a playground. Reach **Sant Martí church** and go right on Carrer d'Alfons Sala and then turn right again onto Carrer de la Coma and arrive at the **information centre**.

Variant

If you would prefer to descend through forest, go left from the junction towards Coves de Mura; this path is also marked with signs for SL-C 69.

Descend among trees and at the junction go right steeply downhill. Continue straight on to Mura by the signpost. There is an option to make a detour to **Cova de Mura** on the right, about 150 metres from the path. If you intend to visit the cave you need to book a guided tour. For more information visit or call the Mura Information Centre.

Descend on the rocky path and shortly after follow a ledge with some great views of the wooded mountainside.

Entrance to Cova de Mura

The houses of Mura come into view across the valley

Reach and cross a track and continue straight on downhill on its other side on the SL-C 69 trail towards 'Centre d'Informació de Mura'. Follow the path in the streambed. Ignore a path on the left and continue straight on with a rock wall on your left. Shortly after, the houses of Mura on the hillside come into view. At the junction continue left downhill to Mura on the SL-C 69 marked path and a few minutes later, at the next junction, continue straight on towards Mura. Follow the path marked with SL-C 69 and ignore other paths. As you descend you can see the houses of Mura across the valley on your right.

Ignore the path on the left marked with SL-C 66 to Font de la Coma and continue straight on towards the Centre d'Informació de Mura. A few metres after this sign, take the path on the right downhill and then go left just before reaching the houses. Arrive on a tarmac road, go right, cross the streambed and then turn right. Follow the signs to the **information centre**.

MONTSERRAT NATURAL PARK

A birds-eye view of Montserrat Monastery (Walk 23)

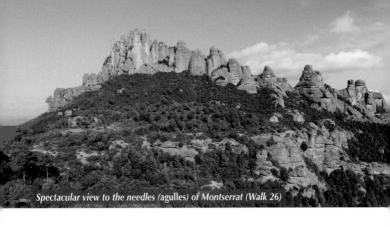
Spectacular view to the needles (agulles) of Montserrat (Walk 26)

MONTSERRAT NATURAL PARK

Montserrat means 'serrated' mountains in Catalan and the name defines the mountain range perfectly. While many people choose to take the scenic cable car ride from Monistrol de Montserrat to the monastery, walkers should climb the impressive trail from the village (Walk 22). The Benedictine monastery – founded in the 11th century and enshrining the Virgin of Montserrat – was rebuilt during the 19th–20th centuries and is still a functioning monastery.

The Montserrat range was declared a natural park in 1987 and there are numerous marked and unmarked hiking trails criss-crossing the mountains. There is a jaw-dropping 360-degree panorama from the highest peak, Sant Jeroni (Walk 23), but take any of the trails among the rock needles (*agulles*) and your steps will be accompanied by far-reaching dramatic views. There is a hotel near the monastery building but you can stay in Monistrol de Montserrat or Collbató if you want to be close to the trails. Manresa is also close enough to explore the trails and the town has everything that a walker might need. Wine production has always been important in the area; grapes were grown on the terraced vineyards and some of these old terraces can still be seen today. If you want to sample the local wine, head to Oller del Mas winery. The estate dates back to the 10th century and you can book a wine tasting tour and/or stay in one of the modern cabins dotted around the estate (see Appendix C).

There are regular trains to Monistrol de Montserrat from Barcelona and Manresa. The Sagalés and Hispano Igualadina bus companies operate local buses in the area:

https://www.monbus.es/en
https://www.sagales.com/

WALK 22

Montserrat Monastery from
Monistrol de Montserrat

Start/finish	Monistrol de Montserrat, Plaça de la Font Gran, N41.609518, E1.842376
Distance	8.5km
Total ascent/descent	670m
Grade	2
Time	3hr plus allow extra time for the monastery.
Refreshments	Cafés and restaurants in Monistrol de Montserrat. Café and restaurant near the monastery.
Access	There is a small car park near Plaça de la Font Gran. The walk itself starts from the main square.

The monastery is a popular destination for day trippers from Barcelona and while some of the visitors arrive by funicular, the most rewarding approach is to follow a section of the GR 96 long-distance trail from the village of Monistrol de Monsterrat. It is well signposted and easy to follow. However, there are some very steep sections with numerous steps to climb. On the return leg, the trail described follows a section of the GR 5 long-distance trail with some steep steps to descend.

From the map board on Carrer de la Font Gran in Monistrol de Montserrat, follow the red/white GR signs. Reach a road and carefully cross over, and continue on the other side. (This section of the trail is marked with signs for the GR 5, GR 96 and Els 3 Monts IP-6.) Ascend by a house. Ignore a path (marked with 'X') on your left, continue alongside a fence and shortly pass a farm. Follow the red/white and green/red stripes uphill ignoring any path marked with 'X'. You already have a good view of the village. Arrive on a track (**Camí de les Aigües**, 265m) about 15min from the village and go left. ▶ A few minutes later the GR 5 and GR 96 split. Go right on the

The emblematic rock formations dominate the scenery.

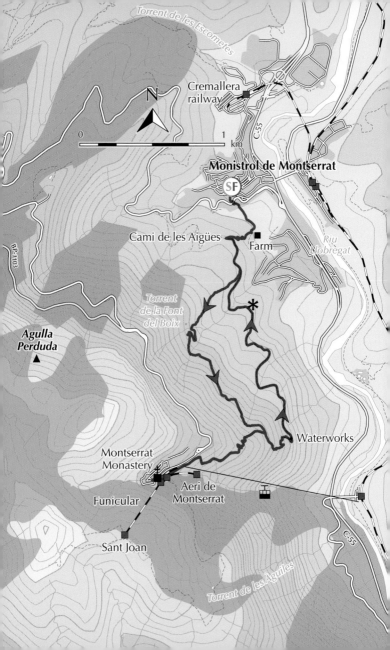

N

0   1
                                    km

Torrent de les Escometes

Cremallera railway

C-55

Monistrol de Montserrat

SF

Cami de les Aigües

Farm

Riu Llobregat

Torrent de la Font del Boix

BP-1103

Agulla Perduda

Waterworks

Montserrat Monastery

Funicular

Aeri de Montserrat

Sant Joan

C-55

Torrent de les Aguiles

GR 96 path (you will return to this junction from the GR 5). Follow the stony path steeply uphill towards the rocks.

At **Torrent de la Font del Boix** (380m) continue uphill and soon you might notice the rack railway on the steep mountainside. The shrub-lined path meanders uphill. At the next junction go right uphill along a pipeline. From the monastery you will return to this junction. The GR 5 route rejoins and from here it shares the path with the GR 96 again. You can also see signs for the Els 3 Monts trail. This is a steep section with some steps. Arrive on a paved path with a signpost about 1hr 20min from Monistrol de Montserrat. Go right uphill and soon see the

Note: map scale is 1:25,000

Rocky path going steeply uphill

MONASTERY OF MONTSERRAT

Aeri de Montserrat and the monastery above

According to legend the statue of the Virgin of Montserrat was found in AD880 in the Montserrat mountains. That was the start of the cult of the Moreneta virgin in four earlier hermitages: Santa Maria, Sant Iscle, Sant Pere and Sant Martí in the ninth century.

Oliba, Abbot of Ripoll and Bishop of Vic, founded a new monastery at the hermitage of Santa Maria de Montserrat in 1025. During the 12th and 13th centuries a Romanesque church was built and pilgrims started to visit Montserrat.

Napoleon's troops burnt down the building twice, in 1811 and in 1812, and many of the treasures were taken. It was then rebuilt in the 19th century and then in the 20th century.The monastery enshrines Our Lady of Montserrat, one of the black Madonnas of Europe. The Catalan name, *La Morenata*, means 'the little dark one'.

The monastery celebrated 1000 years of existence in 1880 and Pope Leo XIII proclaimed the Virgin of Montserrat patron of Catalunya in 1881. The Virgin of Montserrat (Our Lady of Montserrat) and Sant Jordi (Saint George) are the patron saints of Catalunya.

During the Franco era the monastery became the symbol of resistance and a sanctuary for scholars, artists, students and politicians, and despite the restrictions on the use of Catalan language the publishing house, the Publicacions de l'Abadia de Montserrat, continued to publish in Catalan.

Today it is still a functioning monastery with about 70 monks and the famous Boys' Choir, which performs during religious ceremonies, is one of the oldest in Europe.

cable car. About 10min later arrive at Aeri de Montserrat station and follow the paved path to the **monastery**.

From the information centre follow the paved path to Aeri de Montserrat station and then continue downhill following the GR red/white signs. At the junction with a signpost, go left on the GR 5 and GR 96 marked path (retracing the way you came up). There are some steps and then you zigzag downhill among shrubs and at the junction where the GR 96 goes left, go right on the GR 5 path. There are some views of the snaking Llobregat river on the left as you follow the path on the mountainside. Descend steeply on steps and pass a **waterworks building** (Estació elevadora d'aigua potable, 425m) at the bottom of the steps.

Shortly after follow a wider path. Ignore a path on the right and continue downhill towards Monistrol de Montserrat. Towering rocks dominate the scenery on your left and you can also see the houses of Monistrol de Montserrat. Notice a viewpoint with a flag on your right in the near distance.

At the junction with a signpost (where the GR 96 joins from the left) continue straight on to Monistrol de Montserrat. Leave this wide path to the right, on a path with a 'Monistrol' sign. Zigzag downhill and then descend alongside a fence, passing a farm building. Reach a road, cross over and arrive back at **Monistrol de Montserrat**.

WALK 23

Sant Jeroni

Start/finish	Monastir de Montserrat (Montserrat Monastery), N41.592154, E1.835356
Distance	10.5km
Total ascent/descent	680m
Grade	3
Time	3hr 30min–4hr
Refreshments	Café, restaurant and small supermarket near the monastery.
Access	The BP-1121 road leads to a large car park near the monastery. Parking for a day will cost you €6.50. Alternatively, you can take the funicular from outside Monistrol de Montserrat (www.aeridemontserrat.com). From Monistrol de Montserrat you can also choose to take the rack railway, the Cremallera de Montserrat.

Fascinating pinnacles dominate the scenery from this popular walk, and from the peak of Jeroni, on a clear day, you will be greeted with views all the way to the Pyrenees. The route starts from the monastery and climbs to the highest point of the Montserrat range. It is a well-signposted, well-trodden trail. However, there are many sets of steps – some of them steep – along the way.

From the square, start on the steps next to the statue of Oliba. Climb the two sets of steps, go right by a shrine and cross a bridge towards Sant Jeroni. There are a lot of steps to be climbed during the first section of the walk. Shortly, follow a paved path and climb another set of steps alongside a rock wall. Crossing a wooden bridge, ascend more steps.

At Plaça de Santa Anna (895m) continue towards Sant Jeroni ignoring a path on the left (which goes towards the Funicular de Sant Joan). Climb another set of

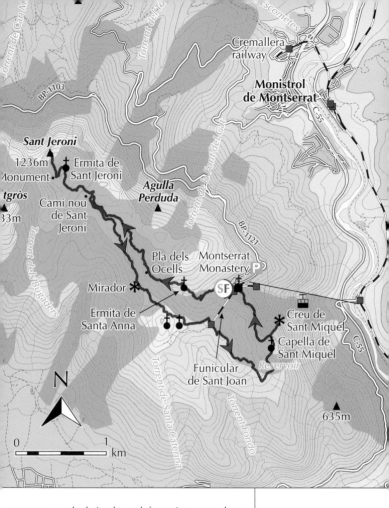

steep steps and admire the rock formations around you.
Shortly the antennas on one of the peaks in the distance
become visible. Pass a stone obelisk and arrive at **Pla dels
Ocells** (930m). Ignore a path on the left, and continue
straight on. Shortly after, there are some further steps and
then follow the forest path alongside a streambed.

Pass a monument
dedicated to Jacint
Verdaguer, one of
the greatest poets
of Catalunya.

At Cami nou de Sant Jeroni (1050m), go right uphill initially on a concrete path. This then becomes a stony path with a rock face on one side and railings on the other. At Cami dels Francesos (1125m), ignore the path on the left (going to El Brull/Collbató) and continue straight on to Sant Jeroni. Go left by **Ermita de Sant Jeroni**. Ascend some steps and enjoy some great views of the rock 'needles'. ◀ Reach the peak of **Sant Jeroni** after another set of steps, about 1hr 30min from the monastery. The unobstructed panorama is dominated by jagged peaks and rock pinnacles.

From the peak retrace your steps to Ermita San Jeroni and then go right and follow the path downhill back to the junction at **Cami nou de Sant Jeroni** (where you arrived from the left on your ascent). Go right on the path marked as 'Monastir de Montserrat per Sant Miquel'. Descend on the stony forest path. Shortly you can enjoy further views of the rounded rock needles around you. This is an easy section and you might want to spend some time admiring the amazing scenery. Notice some steps on the right which take you up to a viewing platform (*mirador*) from where you can enjoy further views.

The path then runs along a ledge with a railing and you can see the buildings of the monastery standing proudly by the cliffs down below. Descend and ignore a path to Santa Magdalena on the right at Regió de Santa Magdalena (1010m). Continue straight downhill and after some steps the path becomes paved. Ignoring a path on the left, continue downhill and arrive at the Funicular de Sant Joan. Go left downhill on the paved path. (From here you could take the funicular back to the monastery.)

Follow this paved path downhill with some views. Pass a reservoir on your left and about 20min after the funicular station, pass **Capella de Sant Miquel** and continue downhill. Notice a path on the right-hand side heading to the Creu de Sant Miquel viewpoint; the rocky outcrop is a perfect spot to enjoy views of the monastery complex. At the next junction continue downhill, passing shrines and art works, and shortly after arrive back at **Montserrat Monastery**.

The path gets easier as you get closer to the funicular

WALK 24
Ermita de Sant Joan

Start/finish	Monastir de Montserrat, statue of Oliba, N41.592154, E1.835356
Distance	6.5km
Total ascent/descent	600m
Grade	2
Time	2hr 30min
Refreshments	Café and restaurant near the monastery.
Access	The BP-1121 road leads to a large car park near the monastery. Parking for a day will cost you €6.50. Alternatively you can take the funicular from Monistrol de Montserrat (www.aeridemontserrat.com). From Monistrol de Montserrat you can also choose to take the rack railway, the Cremallera de Montserrat.

This walk is a perfect alternative if you don't want to climb the highest peak, Sant Jeroni, but still want to enjoy some spectacular views of the iconic rock formations of the Montserrat. The first and the final sections of the trail are shared with Walk 23; however, the rest of the trail offers some very different views. You will pass the ruins of several hermitages and can enjoy a bird's eye view of the monastery.

From the statue of Oliba climb the two sets of steps and go right by a shrine, towards Sant Jeroni. After crossing the bridge climb the steps. Shortly follow a paved path and climb another set of steps alongside a rock wall. Crossing a wooden bridge, climb some more steps.

At Plaça de Santa Anna (895m) go left towards Funicular de Sant Joan (ignoring the other path to Sant Jeroni). Pass the ruins of **Ermita de Santa Anna**. There are some amazing views; soon you can spot the monastery buildings hugged by rocks down below. On a clear day you can make out the silhouettes of La Mola and Montcau in the distance. Ascend the stony path and about 40min from the monastery, at the first of several signposts for Regió de Santa Magdalena (955m), go left towards Funicular de Sant Joan and a few metres later turn right uphill onto a less-trodden path. Zigzag steeply uphill for a few minutes and go right when you reach a more obvious path. Shortly after at the Regió de Santa Magdalena (1010m) signpost, take the path towards Santa Magdalena going steeply uphill, ignoring a path on the right. Climb the steep rocky path and occasional steep stone steps. At Regió de Santa Magdalena (1070m)

Note: map scale is 1:25,000

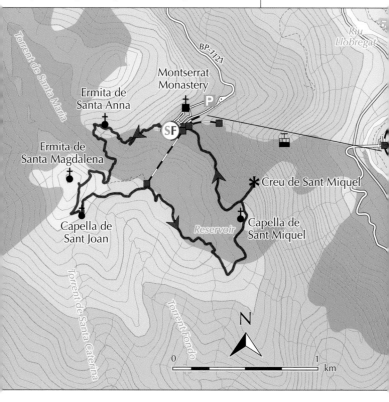

Brilliant views from Ermita de Santa Magdalena

go right to make a short detour to the ruins of **Ermita de Santa Magdalena** and just a little further on, reach a great viewpoint.

The **hermitage** was accessible via a series of steep steps cut into the rocks, and for this reason the older hermits and monks avoided it. Like many of the hermitages in the Montserrat it was abandoned in 1812.

From Regió de Santa Magdalena (1070m) take the path towards Funicular de Sant Joan and descend on stone steps. Take the path on the rock ledge by a rock wall on the right (the other path continues steeply downhill). This is a very narrow path on the ledge with a railing on your left. There are some great views. Passing the ruins of Ermita de Sant Onofre descend on steps and follow the path downhill; you can see a chapel and the paved path. Pass the ruins of Ermita de Sant Joan and follow the paved path downhill passing **Capella de Sant Joan**. Ignore stairs on the left and continue downhill on the path.

Soon arrive at the Funicular de Sant Joan. Pass the station and continue downhill on the paved path. You will be following this paved path downhill with some far-reaching views. Pass a reservoir on your left and about 20min after the funicular station pass **Capella de Sant Miquel**. Notice a path on the right-hand side of the path which takes you to a rocky outcrop, **Creu de Sant Miquel**, with perfect views towards the monastery complex. At the junction continue downhill. Pass shrines and some art works and shortly after arrive back at the square near **Montserrat Monastery**.

Pass the ruins of Ermita de Sant Joan

WALK 25
Roca Foradada and Cami de la Portella

Start/finish	Coll Can Maçana car park, N41.609738, E1.767852
Distance	9km
Total ascent/descent	850m
Grade	3 (There are possible route-finding difficulties, and also a very steep section at Canal de Miracle.)
Time	3hr 30min–4hr
Refreshments	None
Access	Can Maçana car park is located on the BP-1101 road. The car park is free on weekdays but you have to pay €4 for a day at weekends (price is correct as of 2021).

Some stunning views of striking rock formations accompany you on this walk. The trail initially follows the well-trodden GR 172 trail and gives you an option to climb to the popular Roca Foradada, a rock window where you can enjoy some amazing views. The trail then follows some lesser-used paths before joining the PR-C 78 trail, also known as the Cami de la Portella.

From the car park start uphill by the information board and then go through a barrier and immediately after that, at a junction, go left uphill on the GR 172 track. A few minutes later there is a viewpoint on your left. Follow the track towards the rocks. About 10–15min from the car park notice a trail with signs on the right-hand side. You can take that path to the ruins of **Sant Pau Vell church**. From the ruins there are some incredible views of the rock needles (*agulles*). ◄

Allow at least an extra 15min for the detour to the church.

> **Sant Pau Vell church** was built in the 11th century and then went through modifications during the 14th century. It stood beside the Castell de la Guàrdia, but unfortunately nothing but a few stones remain of the castle today.

Continue on the GR 172 track and at the next junction carry straight on towards Monastir de Montserrat. Ignore a path on the left and continue downhill on the stony track. At the junction at **Collet de Guirló** (797m) continue straight on, on the GR 172 trail. (You will return to this junction from the path on the right.) Shortly after, the rock window (Roca Foradada) comes into view as you follow the undulating path. Ignore a faint path on the right and continue on the well-trodden path. At the next small junction just before reaching the base of the rock face, **La Cadireta**, take the steep path on the right, then climb on rocks for a few minutes and arrive at **Roca Foradada**.

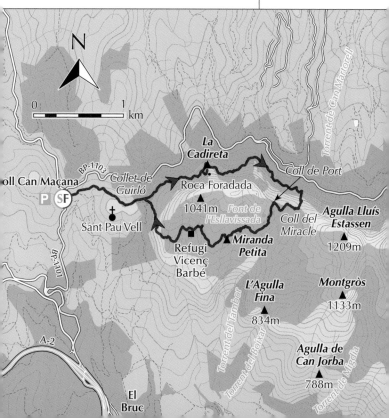

Roca Foradada

Enjoy the views and then retrace your steps to the junction and continue on the GR 172 path. It skirts around La Cadireta, a popular climbing spot. At Els Frares Encantats (837m), go left downhill towards Monastir de Montserrat. ▶ Descend on the narrow path and at Els Frares Eucantats (752m), ignore the path on the left going down to the main road (BP-1103) and continue straight on. Follow the undulating path marked with red/white GR signs.

At Canal del Miracle (810m) leave the GR 172 trail on the narrow path to the right. Follow the blue paint marks on rocks. Climb steeply uphill, often holding onto rocks and roots with your hands. You will be climbing for about 15–20min; look out for and follow the blue paint marks as the route might not be obvious here. Reaching a path at the foot of the rocks, keep right and follow the blue painted marks. Shortly after emerge onto a more obvious path (**Coll del Miracle**) and go right. This section of the trail is part of the PR-C 78 trail and marked with yellow/white signs. The scenery is dominated by typically rounded rocks. Pass by some overhanging rocks. At **Coll de Port** (973m) take the PR-C 78 trail on the left towards Refugi Vicenç Barbé. (Ignore the other sign at Coll de Port (975m) which marks the beginning of a more technical route.)

If you look back you can see the rock window with La Cadireta on its right.

The scenery is dominated by rounded rocks

Sweeping views from Roca Foradada

Descend first and then follow the rocky path uphill passing a small cave and **Font de l'Esllavissada** on your right. Ignore any unmarked trails and paths that are marked with a yellow/white 'X', and follow the yellow/white PR-C signs for about 30min.

At Canal Ampla (803m) go left towards Refugi Vicenç Barbé and Can Maçana. A few minutes later arrive at **Refugi Vicenç Barbé**. Continue right with the building on your left and look out for waymarkers. Descend with some great views and ignore a path on the left. The path crosses over a streambed. At the junction (Les Agulles, 855m) continue straight on to Can Maçana. Follow the narrow path squeezed between the rocks, ignoring a path marked with red on your right. The channel-like path leads steeply downhill between Roca Gran de la Portella and Portella Petita. Climb down on rocks and then it becomes an easy rocky path. Soon the ruins of a church on the nearby mountain become visible, and shortly after arrive back at the junction (Collet de Guirló). Turn left and about 10min later arrive back at the **car park**.

WALK 26

Els Pallers

Start/finish	Coll Can Maçana car park, N41.609738, E1.767852
Distance	8km
Total ascent/descent	330m
Grade	3 (some route-finding difficulties)
Time	2hr 30min
Refreshments	None
Access	Can Maçana car park is located on the BP-1101 road, 4.5km north of El Bruc. The car park is free on weekdays but you have to pay €4 for a day at the weekend (price is correct as of 2021).

During this spectacular walk you can admire the fascinating rock 'needles' from different angles and also have some great views towards El Bruc. There is also an opportunity for a short detour to the ruins of Sant Pau Vell church. There is an information point and plenty of picnic tables at Can Maçana.

From the parking area start uphill by the information board and then go through a barrier and immediately after, at the junction, go left uphill on the GR 172 track. A few minutes later there is a viewpoint on your left. Follow the track towards the rocks. About 10–15min from car park notice a trail with signs on the right-hand side. You can take that path to the ruins of **Sant Pau Vell church**. From the ruins there are some spectacular views of the needles (*agulles*) of Montserrat. Allow at least an extra 15min for the detour to the church.

> **Sant Pau Vell church** was built in the 11th century and then went through modifications during the 14th century. The church was built next to the Castell de la Guàrdia but unfortunately nothing but some scattered rocks remain of the castle today.

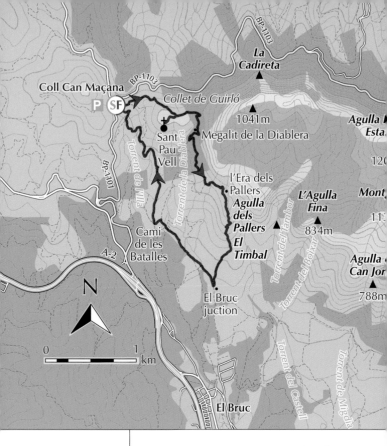

Continue on the GR 172 towards Refugi Vicenç Barbé and at the next junction take the track on the right downhill towards El Bruc. The landscape is dominated by towering rock formations. Descend steeply and then pass a sign: 'Zona Arqueològica del torrent de la Diablera'. This marks an area where some neolithic structures/remains were found (**Megalit de la Diablera**). There is a streambed by the track on the right-hand side. Shortly notice a sign marking a narrow path on the right. Just behind the huge boulders there is a path leading to a natural rock shelter which is only a few metres off the track. Descend on the track with some views towards the rock needles now on your left.

At the junction turn left towards Refugi Vicenç Barbé with towering rocks on your left and views of pine-covered hillside on your right. Reach a junction and go left on the PR-C 78 trail towards Refugi Vicenç Barbé. Ascend on the narrow rocky path among shrubs. Shortly after reach a small coll (**l'Era dels Pallers**), at about 3km from Can Maçana, and turn right towards the rocks (Els Pallers). As you follow the narrow path, notice some green marks painted on rocks. The rounded *agulles* are behind you at this point, looking like a group of chimneys. Follow the very narrow path on the right side of the rocks. Take care as the path is very narrow and it is often no more than a slippery ledge. It is also overgrown in places. Keeping the rocks on your left, look out for faint green paint marks. There are some views towards El Bruc.

On reaching the last huge rock with a hole go left. Walk between the huge rock with a hole and a smaller rock formation, and immediately after turn right downhill.

On reaching the last huge rock with a hole go left

Take care as you make the steep descent as it can be slippery. The path might be less obvious here; look out for very faint yellow marks painted on rocks, and you might also spot some green/blue marks. Descend steeply downhill in the gully for about 10min and then the path becomes more obvious. Continue to descend following yellow paint marks. Upon reaching a clearing with a rock cairn continue straight on, and at a small path junction with another rock cairn go right downhill among shrubs. The path soon widens and runs through a wooded area with pine trees. Notice an information board and continue on the wide path (ignoring the path by the board). There is an olive grove on the left side of the path.

At the junction (**El Bruc**) go right towards Can Maçana. ◄ Follow the forest track, passing a house, and then leave the track to the right on a path. Shortly after reach a track and go right. Ignore a path on the left going to the olive grove and continue straight on with some views towards the rugged rocks on your right. At a junction continue straight on, and a few minutes later at a junction with signs turn left towards Can Maçana. Immediately after, at the next junction with signs, go right to Can Maçana (35min from here).

Don't be alarmed by the time noted on some of the signs. There are many different trails in the area, so the signs might refer to the time for a different route.

This last section of the trail is part of the Camí de les Batalles trail. You can enjoy some views back towards Els Pallers. Pine forest populates this area and soon you can spot the ruins of Sant Pau Vell. At the junction go left towards Can Maçana on the Camí de les Batalles trail and follow the track uphill. When the track splits go left. Ignore a path on the left and bend right steeply uphill. At the next junction follow the signs for Camí de les Batalles to the left and arrive back at the bottom of the **car park**.

WALK 27

Montserrat Monastery from Collbató

Start/finish	Collbató, Coves del Salnitre car park, N41.572656, E1.829068
Distance	12km (there and back)
Total ascent/descent	700m
Grade	2
Time	4hr–4hr 30min
Refreshments	Café, restaurant and shop by the monastery.
Access	From the B-112 road just outside of Collbató, take the road towards Coves de Collbató.

This there-and-back route offers an amazing way to reach the monastery with some fantastic views, and is less steep than the one from Monistrol de Montserrat. The trail follows some well-trodden paths, making use of parts of the GR 172 and the GR 5 long-distance trails. From the monastery you can continue down to Monistrol de Montserrat (see Walk 22) or alternatively retrace your steps to Collbató. You can also extend the day with a visit to the caves.

From the car park climb the steps by the information board and shortly after pass another information board about the local vegetation. Reach a tarmac road, turn right and then take the left branch of the tarmac road. There are red/white GR signs and shortly after reach a parking area at the end of the tarmac road. There is a signpost here. You will be following the 'Monastir de Montserrat pel cami de la Santa Cova' trail.

Climb the steps from the car park to **Coves del Salnitre**. (If you want to visit the cave you have to pre-book a tour online on www.collbato.cat/coves-de-montserrat.htm.) The trail continues to Monastir de Montserrat. There are some views towards tree-covered hills and the path runs alongside a steep rock wall. Look out for a small cave on the left-hand side. Follow the ledge with the rock wall on the left. Ignore any side paths and arrive at a junction with a signpost about 30–40min from Coves del Salnitre. Continue towards Monastir de Montserrat (1hr 15min) on the GR 5/GR 172 trail. As you zigzag uphill, the scenery is dominated by towering rocks that are somewhat different on this

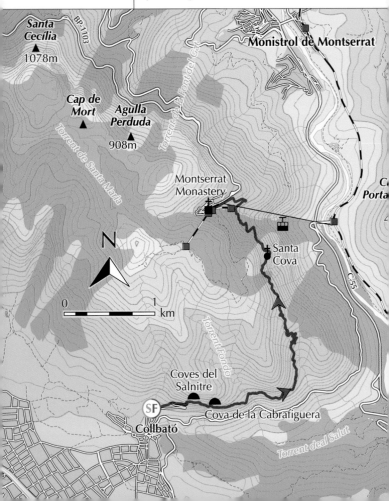

side of the mountains. The Llobregat river comes into view down below. Follow the path uphill with some excellent views of rugged rocky peaks for about 30min and arrive at the next junction with a signpost. The trail divides here. Take the GR 5.1 trail on the right to 'Monastir de Montserrat pel camida la Santa Cova'. (The GR 5 also continues to the monastery but on the Cami de Sant Miquel route.)

Santa Cova church with its high supporting walls soon comes into view. Shortly after the path skirts below the church building and the Mirador the Montserrat (viewpoint and restaurant) comes into view on the mountainside. Emerge onto a surfaced path by a signpost about 30min from the junction where the path split. Go left to visit **Santa Cova church** (about 100 metres).

Follow the path uphill with excellent views of the rugged rocky scenery

SANTA COVA

According to legend, in AD880 two young shepherds saw a light descend from heaven and settle halfway up Montserrat mountain. The light appeared a few more times, always accompanied by a beautiful song. When the bishop of Manresa heard about the appearance of the light he went to Montserrat. A grotto with an icon of the Virgin Mary was found, but when the bishop and his people tried to take the icon to Manresa, it became too heavy. It was taken as a sign that the icon should be worshipped in Montserrat.

The 17th-century chapel was built on the spot where the vision appeared, under an overhanging rock. Next to the altar you can see the reproduction of the Virgin.

After visiting the church take the paved path to Monastir de Montserrat (pel Cami del Rosary).

This is also known as the **Monumental Rosary of Montserrat**. The 15 religious artworks along the way represent the 15 mysteries of the rosary. Even Gaudí contributed to this project: he designed *The First Mystery of Glory, the Resurrection of Jesus*.

Pass a large crucifix and then shortly after pass the building of the Funicular Al Monestir (Santa Cova). Continue on the paved path and at the junction go left uphill. About 10min later arrive at Aeri de Montserrat station and continue to **Montserrat Monastery**. After visiting, retrace your steps to **Collbató**.

PENEDÈS AND GARRAF NATURAL PARK

The last stretch of the path on Walk 32 before you get back to La Joncosa del Montmell

Walk 28 follows red and white waymarks across the hills

PENEDÈS AND GARRAF NATURAL PARK

Penedès and the Garraf Natural Park might not have high mountains, but the areas offer a variety of trails leading to castle ruins (Walk 30) or shaded river gorges (Walk 31), or traverse ridges with extensive views (Walk 32). The Penedès is a Spanish Denominacion de Origen Protegida (DOP) region for its fine wines in Catalunya. There are endless vineyards which have produced delicious wine since ancient times so not surprisingly the Penedès is considered one of the best wine-producing regions. The area is better known for its Cava production although some great oak-aged reds are also made in the region. Many wineries offer wine tasting tours. Vilafranca del Penedès, the capital of the comarca of Alt Penedès, is a bustling town where many of the wines of the region can be sampled. (For more information about the area and some cellar and wine tours visit www.penedesturisme.cat.)

South of Barcelona, the coastal towns are popular with tourists during the summer months. However, they can be a good base if you want to explore the Garraf Natural Park but don't want to stay in Barcelona. There are some extensive views towards the coast and Barcelona (Walk 28), and you can go for a gentle walk near the abandoned village of Jafra (Walk 29). Accommodation can be found in Vilafranca del Penedès and for those looking for something different, some of the wineries also offer rooms. If you want to base yourself in one of the smaller towns in the Penedès, it is easier to explore the trails described in this book with your own transport.

Vilafranca really comes alive during festivals. Sant Félix day is an important day in the town, celebrating the patron saint of Vilafrance. Magnificent *castells* (human towers) are built on Plaça de la Vila attracting great number of spectators.

There are regular trains to Vilafranca del Penedès, Castelldefels, Garraf, Sitges and Vilanova i la Geltrú from Barcelona. The Bus Garraf provides local transport. The Hispano Igualadina and Autocars del Penedès companies also serve some routes in the Penedès area:

https://www.busgarraf.cat/en/
https://autocarsdelpenedes.com/
https://www.monbus.es/en

WALK 28
Garraf to Bruguers

Start	Garraf railway station, N41.255476, E1.903434
Finish	Ermita de Bruguers, Bruguers
Distance	16km
Total ascent	780m
Total descent	500m
Grade	2
Time	4hr 30min–5hr
Refreshments	Two restaurants at the end of the trail near Ermita de Bruguers.
Access	Garraf is on the train line that runs along the coast. From Sitges or from Barcelona you can reach Garraf on the C-31 road. If you intend to return to Garraf take the 902 bus to Gavà. From Gavà take a train back to Garraf. The bus stop is next to the restaurant (near the church) on the BV-2041 road.

The first section of this linear trail offers magnificent views of the Balearic Sea and the coastline, and the route then takes you through the rugged limestone landscape of the Garraf Natural Park. From La Morella enjoy some fine views towards Barcelona. At the final section pass the ruins of Castell d'Eramprunyá before reaching the 13th-century church, Ermita de Bruguers. The route follows a section of the GR 92 long-distance trail, so it is well signposted with red/white stripes.

From the train station follow Carrer Estació and then Avinguda del Comte Güell. After the sport club take the underpass that takes you under the C-31 road. Emerging on the other side go right and follow the red/white stripes along the C-31 road for about 200 metres. Please take extra care as you will be walking along a very busy road! At the junction spot the red/white sign on the crash barrier and leave the road on the path on the left just after

Puig de les
Agulles
552m

Pic de
l'Àliga
534m

Puig
Martí
508m

La
Morella
594m

La
Bena
555m

El
Rascler
574m

Puig
de l'Olla
429m

• Avenc Asensio

• Avenc de
la Silvia

Pla de
Querol

P

Llacsí
363m

La Pleta

P

N

Turó d
Covafu
135m

Dog shelter •

0   1
km

• Quarry fence

C-32

C-31

C-32

S

Railway
station

Garraf

C-31

Map continues
on page 155

the junction. The path runs parallel to the road at first and it is frequently marked with red/white stripes. Soon the path enters the Parc del Garraf. Ignore a path on the right (which goes down to a car park by the road) and continue straight on. Shortly after go left towards La Pleta and La Morella and follow the signs. As you zigzag uphill on the well-trodden path, ignoring any other paths, there are some great views towards the Balearic Sea and the coastal towns of Castelldefels and Garraf.

Rosemary and other low shrubs populate the hillside.

▸ Reach a track by a fence with a deep quarry behind it, and go left. Walk alongside the fence of the quarry. The deep gorge of Fondo de les Coves with its numerous hidden caves and caverns stretches on the left. You can spot a radar dome on a mountain top near La Morella. At the end of the fence, just after a dog shelter, leave the track to the left on the marked path that might be slightly overgrown. Follow the signs and a few minutes later reach and cross a tarmac road. The GR 92 trail continues on the other side of the road. Pass a chain barrier by a map board. Follow the wide path and go left to La Pleta.

Great views towards the Balearic Sea

Reach **La Pleta** about 1hr 40min from Garraf. The building was designed by the architect Francesc Berenguer and was owned by the Güell family. Today it serves as the Garraf Park Office and Information Centre, where you can pick up some leaflets about the natural park.

Join the narrow tarmac road near the building and go right. Follow the road for about 1.5km to **Pla de Querol car park**. From the parking area go right on the paved road marked with a sign for the GR 92 towards La Morella. Follow the paved road for about 500 metres and then leave the road to the right on the red/white marked path. This narrow path among shrubs passes some deep chasms. These are marked but take extra care and don't wander off the path!

About 10–15min later arrive back on the paved road. Go right and then immediately right again on a paved track towards La Morella. A few minutes later leave the track to the left by the fence and continue on the GR 92 trail. Pass a ruined house and about 40min from Pla de

Querol car park, at the junction, go right uphill. Follow the path to the small peak of **La Morella** (594m) with an information board about birds that you might spot. Enjoy the views of the mountains of Garraf Natural Park and the sea. You might spot Castell d'Eramprunyá perched on rocks, as well as Montjuïc in Barcelona and Vilafranca in the Penedès.

From the summit descend on the GR 92 path. Follow the red/white signs and ignore any side paths marked with red/white 'X'. After the descent the path is level for a little while. At the junction go left downhill towards Puig de les Agulles. Continue on the GR 92 trail ignoring the other paths.

At the junction go right following the GR 92 and then at a junction approximately 30–40min from the summit of La Morella continue towards La Clota. From this junction you can make a short detour to **Puig de Les Agulles** (552m) for further great views of the area.

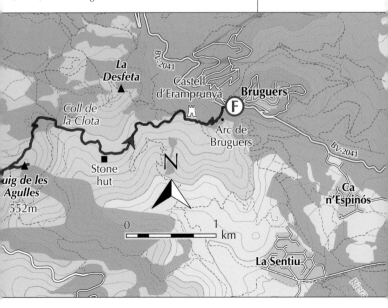

Ignore any other paths and follow the red/white stripes to **Coll de la Clota**, a big junction where several routes meet. Go right and then almost immediately left on the GR 92 path (opposite the cross, Creu de la Clota) towards Castell d'Eramprunyá. ◄ At the junction keep right and about 15min later notice a stone hut on the left. On reaching a dirt track go left following the red/white stripes. When you reach **Castell d'Eramprunyá** continue straight on. Ignore a path on the right and then descend on the rocky path passing the **Arc de Bruguers**. About 50min from La Clota arrive at Ermita de Bruguers in **Bruguers**.

> The **castle** was first mentioned in AD957; however, it probably existed earlier than that. It was part of the defensive system to protect the lands of Llobregat in the 9th and 10th centuries. It was owned by the counts of Barcelona until 1323 when the king, James II, sold it to his treasurer, Pere March. The March family owned the castle until the 16th century. To book a tour email museu@gava.cat tel +34 93 263 96 10.

WALK 29
Jafra circular

Start/finish	Jafra car park, N41.282200, E1.834753
Distance	9km
Total ascent/descent	200m
Grade	1
Time	2hr 30min–3hr
Refreshments	None
Access	Take the road from Castelldefels to Plana Novella. From Avinguda de Plana Novella take Carrer de Migjon to Jafra.

This short walk starts from the abandoned settlement of Jafra (also spelled Jafre). A settlement was first built on this site in the 14th century and there were still 19 people living there in 1960. Today only the crumbling walls of the one-time houses remain. From Jafra follow the forest paths to Cova Negra, peek inside the cave and then walk alongside a river bed. The trail described follows sections of the GR 92.4 and GR 5 trails, as well as the PR-C 37.

From the car park follow the GR 92.4 trail towards Cova Negra and Sant Pere de Ribes. As you descend you can spot green square markings alongside the red/white stripes. Follow the gentle path and notice the fence near the path. ▶ About 15min from the car park arrive at a junction with signs. Cross the track diagonally to the right and continue towards Cova Negra on the GR 92.4 path. Pass a chain barrier and follow the clear path. Follow the GR 92.4 signs, ignoring any unmarked paths, and at the path junction in the riverbed go right towards Sant Pere de Ribas. You will return to this junction after visiting Cova Negra which is about a 2.5km detour.

Cross the Riera de Jafra riverbed and follow the GR 92.4 signs, getting close to a rock wall with a hole (**Forats d'en Bori**). Crossing the riverbed again, follow the rocky

Young pines populate the hillside.

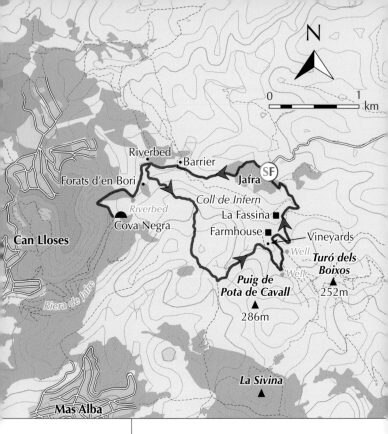

path above and parallel to the Jafra river gorge. Shortly after descend among shrubs. Spot a fire lookout tower on a nearby hill.

Look out for the sign for **Cova Negra** – the cave is a few metres off the path on the left. Go up and take a closer look at the first gallery. The cave is 69 metres in length and specialist equipment is required to explore it.

From the cave return to the junction in the riverbed (about 15min) and go right on the GR 5 trail towards El Coll d'Entreforc/Sitges. This is now part of the route from Sitges to Olivella. Follow the GR 5 for about 30min with views of pine-covered mountains. Notice a boundary fence alongside the path. At the path junction continue straight on, on the GR 5 trail towards Sitges. There are some views of the sea. Descend among trees and at the junction by the electricity pole go left, leaving the GR trail. This path is marked with a red/white 'X'. Shortly a farmhouse comes into view. In the distance you can also spot the ruined buildings of Jafra. Reach a vineyard and continue straight on with the vineyard on your left.

Follow the track, ignoring a path on the right and then on the left. Spot a stone well and then, on reaching a track, go left. Ignore a track going to the farmhouse and descend on the track. Shortly notice some yellow/white stripes marking the PR-C 37 route. Follow the PR-C 37 route ignoring paths on both sides of the track. At the junction with several signs continue uphill towards Jafra and 10min later arrive back at the car park in **Jafra**.

Continue straight on with the vineyard on your left

WALK 30
Castells de Marca trail

Start/finish	Castellet Castle, N41.264556, E1.635827
Distance	28km
Total ascent/descent	700m
Grade	3
Time	8hr–9hr
Refreshments	Café and restaurant in Castellet. Water tap at the picnic site by Olèrdola Castle.
Access	Castellet is located on the BV-2115 road by the Foix reservoir about 15km north-west of Vilanova i la Geltrú.

This trail connects three castles in the region, although it might not be possible to visit all of them. The scenery is dominated by vineyards and old farmhouses with excellent views along the way. This is a long, full day walk so it is important to make sure that you leave early.

There are some great views of the Foix reservoir.

From the castle of Castellet walk to Sant Pere de Castellet. The church has a Romanesque origin and has been documented since the 12th century. ◄ Near the bell tower continue on the paved path alongside the fence and at the Castellet signpost go left on the GR 92.3 trail. This is also marked as the PR-C 148 with yellow/white stripes and with an orange square to Penyafort. Follow the narrow tarmac road downhill passing a parking area. Ignore a track on the left and continue straight on, staying on the paved road signed with an orange square to Penyafort. Reach a road and go right and a few metres later go right on a forest path marked with an orange square.

Pass a chain barrier and continue downhill alongside a vineyard. You can spot some yellow/white signs and when the path splits go left on the path marked with yellow/white stripes and an orange square. Hills and vineyards dominate the scenery. Reach a dirt track and go left and a few metres later go right uphill on a path. Shortly after ignore a path on the right and ascend on the forest path. The hillside is mainly populated by pines. When you reach another path bear right, and then at the junction, turn left as marked with an orange square. There are some views of tree-covered hills and a ruin. Reach a dirt track and go left towards Penyafort.

Arrive at **Torrelletes**, about 30–40min from Castellet. In the village, at the junction with a signpost, continue straight on, on the GR 92.5/92.3 trail (Camí dels Castells towards El Figueral). Continue on Carrer de Santa Magdalena, pass the town hall, carry straight on and then keep left and climb the steps. At the top of the steps go right, leaving the last house of Torrelletes behind by the waterworks. Follow the path by a vineyard and then walk along a smooth limestone path. Reach a track by El Figueral signpost and go left. The orange square signs

Castell de Casellet, the starting point

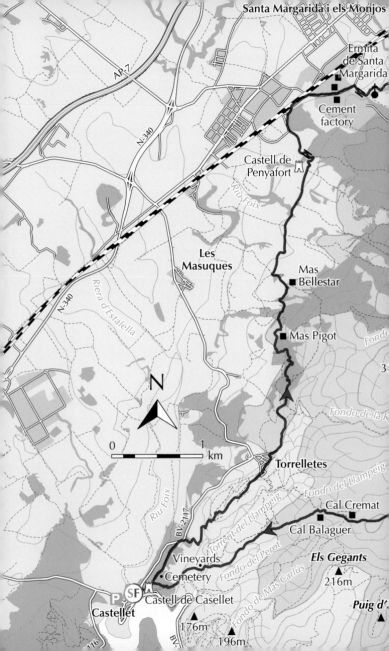

Santa Margarida i els Monjos

Ermita
de Santa
Margarida

Cement
factory

Castell de
Penyafort

Riu Foix

Les
Masuques

Mas
Bellestar

Riera d'Estalella

Mas Pigot

Fondo

N-340

N

Fondo de la K

0   1 km

Torrelletes

Fondo del Llampeig

Cal Cremat

Riu Foix

BV-2117

Torrent del Llampeig

Cal Balaguer

Els Gegants

Vineyards

Fondo del Perot

Cemetery

Fondo de Mas Carlús

▲
216m

Castellet

P SF

Castell de Casellet

▲
176m

▲
196m

Puig d'

BV

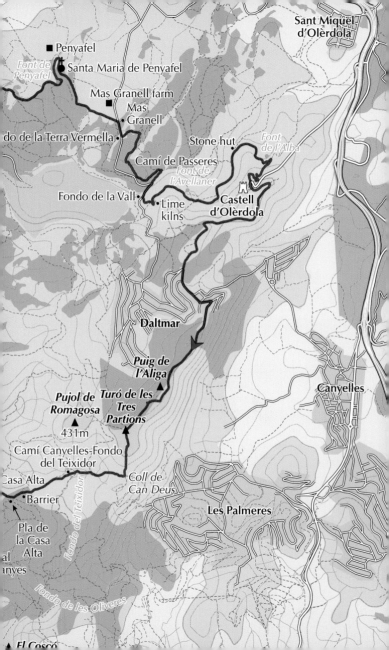

mark the trail all the way to Penyafort. Most of the junctions are signposted and you won't have difficulty finding the next sign. Follow the well-trodden tracks alongside vineyards and then among pines. About 30min from Torrelletes, when the path splits (this is unmarked), go right and shortly after notice the next sign. Emerging from the forest, walk alongside a vineyard and fence and pass a house (**Mas Pigot**) and turn left downhill just before you reach a dirt track.

There are further views of the mountains, villages and vineyards as you descend. Reach a paved track and go left downhill then almost immediately leave the paved track to the right on the track marked with an orange square. Ignore a track on the left and continue straight on uphill.

At the track junction go left towards the buildings (**Mas Bellestar**) and then keep left by the ruins towards Penyafort. ◄ Descend alongside vineyards and at the junction go left downhill. Arrive on a dirt track and go left. At Mas Bellestar-cal Brugal junction go right towards Penyafort.

There are some almond trees here as well as a vineyard.

There are some olive trees by the track as well as more vineyards. Pass a building. At the junction go left and then bear right downhill by Cal Gellego house. Pass another house and continue straight on. There are some views towards the village and some industrial buildings. Notice some SL-C 92 signs alongside the orange squares and reach **Castell de Penyafort**, 1hr 20min from Torreletes.

> **Castell de Penyafort** consists of a medieval tower built in the 11th century, a 17th-century Dominican convent and a 19th-century manor house. Over the centuries, the building complex has been through several modifications. The church was used as a prison during the Spanish Civil War while the residents continued to live in the residential house. Guided tours are available on Sundays (www.penedesturisme.cat). At the time of writing (Aug 2021) the building was under restoration.

From the castle follow the road waymarked with SL-C 92 signs downhill. It crosses over the River Foix and then the SL-C 92 trail leaves the road to the left. The route, however, continues on the road towards the industrial building. At the road junction near the industrial building carry straight on, passing a factory. Continue towards Santa Margarida parallel to the railway, and reach a road and go right. Follow the pavement by this busy road and when the pavement ends, continue on the road for a few hundred metres. Take care as the road is used by lorries transporting goods to and from the factories. It is not an attractive section of the walk but thankfully it is not too long. Spot a yellow/white sign and pass a cement factory. After the cement factory go right towards Castell d'Olèrdola and enter Parc Foix, about 30min from Penyafort Castle.

Cross the River Foix again, walking over a bridge. Pass an information board and some houses and then ignore a track on the right and skirt around the cemetery with the ruins of **Ermita de Santa Margarida**. At the junction take the second path from the right uphill. ▶ Once again vineyards dominate the scenery. Ignore any

Notice a 'Vilafranca del Penedès' sign as a marker for the Camins del Penedès route.

Once again vineyards dominate the scenery after Penyafort

unmarked paths and at the junction continue straight on, on the Camins del Penedès route, ignoring a track on the left. Spot the church tower of Sant Jaume in Moja and the mountains of Montserrat in the distance. At the junction go left downhill and ignore any unmarked side tracks. A church building comes into view. Pass **Penyafel farmhouse** and go right by the signpost, and about 40min after entering Parc Foix arrive at **Santa Maria de Penyafel**.

Passing by the church and its picnic area, continue on the PR-C 148 trail towards Castell d'Olèrdola. At a junction go left and shortly after ignore a track on the right. Continue straight on with a farm on your left and reach **Mas Granell** by the tarmac road. Turn right and follow the road for about 200 metres then leave it to the left by the signpost (Fondo de la Terra Vermella) by the waterworks. There are further views in the direction of Vilafranca with the mountains of Montserrat in the background. At the junction follow the yellow/white sign straight on and immediately keep right on a rocky path downhill. Shortly after you can spot a church across the valley.

Reach a track (near a tarmac road) and then follow the yellow/white signs to the left and downhill. Go right towards Can Castellví by the signpost (**Camí de Passeres**) and pass a farmhouse. Reach the asphalt road and go left downhill. Follow the road for about 200 metres then leave it to the left at the next signpost (Fondo de la Vall-can Castellví), by the 'Parc d'Olèrdola' sign. Follow the track, passing the ruins of an old lime kiln complex (Forns de Calç). Pass a path leading to Font de l'Avellaner. As you follow the track through the valley notice a farmhouse on the hillside on the left. At the junction turn right uphill through a chain barrier and spot a stone hut near the track. Ascend on the broad stony path with further views towards Montserrat. (You can make a short detour to **Font de l'Alba** on the left side of the path.)

Take the path on the right towards Castell de Castellet. (This is signposted with GR 92.3 and PR-C 148 signs as well as the green square to Castell d'Olèrdola.) When the path splits near the tarmac road, go right (without going onto the tarmac). There are some views of

Vilafranca del Penedès with the Monsterrat range in the background as well of the valley you traversed. Reach the tarmac road and the car park by **Castell d'Olèrdola** about an hour after entering Parc d'Olèrdola.

Spot a stone hut near the path

> **Olèrdola castle** has been inhabited since prehistoric times. Today it is a fascinating archaeological site with the remains of Roman buildings as well as a Romanesque church and the castle. In the early Middle Ages the castle controlled the Penedès area; however, its importance declined from the 12th century. The entry fee (2021) is €5. Opening hours are slightly different in every season, but it usually opens at 10:00 with an earlier closing time in the winter. Note that it is closed on Mondays. For detailed opening times and prices check www.penedesturisme.cat.

At the end of the car park continue straight on by the map board. There is a picnic area and water fountain here. Follow the PR-C 148 signs and at the junction go right. Follow the track – signposted with PR-C 148 as well as GR 92.3 – on the mountainside, ignoring a narrow path on the right, for about 30min.

Reach a tarmac road and the first house of Daltmar. Follow the red/white signs on Carrer Parc d'Olèrdola to a roundabout. Carry straight on uphill and then go right on Carrer del Puig de l'Aliga. The route from Daltmar will take approximately 2hr to get back to Castellet.

Leaving the village, the tarmac road becomes a dirt track and there are some views towards the Balearic Sea. Pass the waterworks and descend on the track. Pass some houses and at the junction go left uphill. There are views towards the coastline and Vilanova i la Geltrú. Spot a fire lookout station on the top of Puig de l'Aliga. Follow the GR 92.3 and PR-C 143 signs and at 'Turó de les Tres Partions' signpost continue straight on uphill. At the path junction keep left following the PR-C 143 signs. Pass a chain barrier and follow the path to **Turó de les Tres Partions**. From the top descend on the stony path.

At **Coll de Can Deus** go right downhill. Ignore a path on the right and then on the left and stay on the PR-C 143 trail. At the 'Camí Canyelles–Fondo del Teixidor' signpost carry straight on and a few minutes later by the ruined kiln follow the PR-C 143 signs straight on through a chain barrier. At the dirt track junction, Pla de la Casa Alta, go right and ignore two tracks on the left. At a junction, go left downhill and walk alongside a vineyard. You can see the ruined **La Casa de Alta** on the right. Pass the ruins of **Cal Cassanyes**, a farmhouse. Ignore any side roads and pass **Cal Cremat** (another ruined farmhouse). Shortly after the ruins, go right on a stony path marked with a red/white sign. Pass the ruins of **Cal Balaguer** and then keep left towards Castellet. You can see the houses of Torelletes on the right across the valley as you follow the red/white signs on the ridge. Descend on a narrow path near a vineyard and carry straight on towards Castellet passing some buildings. At the junction go right alongside a fence and pass a house. Shortly after at the junction go right, ignoring any paths, and arrive back at **Castellet** by the church.

WALK 31

Foix river gorge

Start/finish	Santuari de Foix car park, N41.414188, E1.561331
Distance	9.5km
Total ascent/descent	300m
Grade	2
Time	3hr–3hr 30min
Refreshments	None
Access	The car park of Santuari de Foix is about 5km north of Torrelles de Foix. Take Carretera (Ctra.) de la Plana de les Torres from BV-2122 road and then take the road Camí del Santuari de Foix to the parking area.

Follow this charming gorge with long-forgotten ruins, and then spend some time relaxing by the tranquil rock pools. Walk alongside vineyards and admire the amazing panorama from the Santuari de Foix.

From the large parking area, located about 200 metres from the Santuari de Foix, follow the narrow tarmac road downhill. Shortly after notice a path on the right-hand side of the road; this is a short detour to the **Font del Rector**. Continue downhill and the tarmac becomes a dirt track with yellow/white and green/white signs. Reach a junction with a signpost (**Fondo del Rector**) by a vineyard and go right. Turn left by a farmhouse, **Masia Can Rossell**, and pass a chain barrier. Follow the track downhill and at the junction (**Cal Rossell de les Bassegues**), go left towards Gorges del Foix.

Descend through forest passing Font de Cal Rossell. Spot the Santuari de Foix on the hilltop overlooking the river valley. Pass some ruined buildings in the forest. Ignore a path on the left and continue straight on, and about 100 metres later go right on a path marked with a yellow/white 'X' (as you leave the PR-C trail). This

There might be some beehives near the path so take care!

is an SL-C trail. Shortly you will see some green/white signs. ◄ Pass a ruin – once a watermill (**El Molinot**) – and descend on the narrow path. Cross the rocky riverbed and then a few minutes later cross it again over a stone dam. Follow the forest path by the riverbed marked with green/white signs through the gorge, crossing the riverbed and passing two more dams as well as a rock pool. The sound of trickling water and birdsong might accompany you on this section.

Notice some apple and walnut trees by the path and about 50min after you joined the narrow path alongside the riverbed, reach a ruined building (**Moli de la Pineda**). Ignore the path after the ruins and at a junction with a

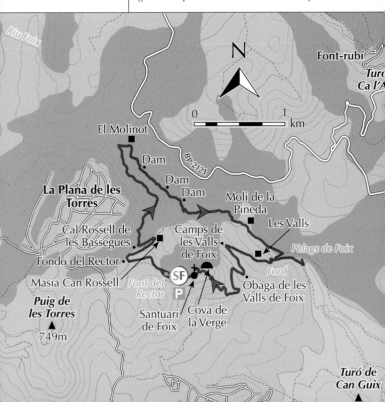

signpost go left alongside the vineyard towards Torrelles de Foix. Reach a track and continue straight on with the vineyard on your right. At the dirt track junction bear right towards Torrelles de Foix and shortly after ford the river. At Guall del Trull (a junction with a signpost) go left. A few minutes later turn sharply left and take the narrow path down to the river. Allow some time in this tranquil place to explore the rock pools (**Pèlags de Foix**) and relax by the small waterfall.

From the river retrace your steps to Guall del Trull junction and keep left. Follow the track alongside the vineyard, and pass some old buildings (**Les Valls**). You can enjoy some views of the hills across the gorge. Ignore a track on the left and continue by the vineyard. ▶ At the track junction, Camps de les Valls de Foix Obaga, go left. (According to the signpost, the Santuari is to the right but that directs you on a different route.) You might be able to spot the buildings of a small settlement (Font Rubi) on the hillside in the distance. At the next intersection (**Obaga de les Valls de Foix**) go right towards the Santuari. Ascend on the track ignoring a path on the left. Shortly after turn

Santuari de Foix

Spot some old ruins in the vineyard.

Explore the rock pools in the gorge

right on a path uphill. Pines and shrubs populate the hillside and on a clear day you can make out the rugged peaks of Montserrat in the distance.

Shortly the building of the Santuari comes into view. At the path junction go right uphill. A steep narrow path heads downhill to the right just before the sanctuary. Take that path to visit a small cave with a shrine inside (**Cova de la Verge**). Otherwise, ignore any paths and continue uphill to reach the **Santuari de Foix**. From the building, you can enjoy the views of Foix village and can see all the way to the sea.

From Santuari de Foix follow the wide track and a few minutes later reach the large **car park** where you started the walk.

The Romanesque church of **Santa Maria de Foix** was part of the Foix castle that stood on the hill overlooking the plain. Not much remains of the castle today. The church was rebuilt several times during the centuries and it was the district's parish church until 1892. The building has a single nave and barrel vaulted ceiling that was recently restored.

WALK 32

El Montmell ridge

Start/finish	Car park in front of Centre Cívic El Montmell in La Joncosa del Montmell, N41.314557, E1.453003
Distance	9km
Total ascent/descent	490m
Grade	2
Time	3hr–3hr 30min
Refreshments	Café and water fountain in the village. Water fountain at the picnic site by Església Nova Sant Miquel.
Access	The car park in La Joncosa del Montmell is 30km west of Vilafranca del Penedès on the TV-2401 road, off the AP-2 motorway.

Traverse a rugged ridge with some extensive views of vineyards and the Balearic Sea. The route begins by skirting around vineyards and then climbs to Sant Miquel church, built in the 12th century. Continue the climb to the ruins of Castell de Montmell.

There are plenty of places to park in front of the Centre Cívic El Montmell. From the parking area take Carrer de l'Om and then turn right onto Calle Major. Follow that road, passing a water fountain and the town hall. Continue straight on and then pass a football pitch and the municipal pool. Leaving the village at the roundabout, continue straight on. Shortly after the roundabout go left, leaving the tarmac road on a dirt track and head towards the hills, alongside vineyards. Soon the castle ruins on the mountain come into view.

At the end of the vineyard the track turns sharply left, but the route continues on a narrower track straight on. Pine trees populate the hillside. Look out for a small wooden BTT (mountain bike track) sign on the right-hand side of the track. Leaving the track go right on this narrow

Leaving Joncosa del Montmell behind

mountain bike trail. When the path splits you can take either branch as they join back together further on.

As you ascend there are further vineyards on the terraced hillside. Reach and cross a dirt track and the path continues on its other side, uphill. Climb towards the railing and arrive back on the dirt track. Cross it and ascend on its other side. Shortly after cross the dirt track again and continue to climb. Pass a concrete water reservoir and cross a dirt track. (If you follow this dirt track to the right it takes you to a picnic site.) Climb some stone steps and pass a spring with a bench. There are some great views towards the village and its vineyards. About 30min after leaving the village, pass some ruins and arrive on a dirt track by the **Església Nova Sant Miquel**. There is a picnic site just below the church, a little further down the dirt track.

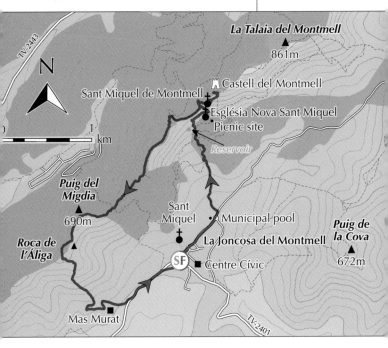

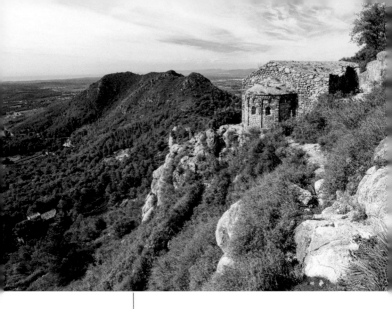

Climb to the
12th-century
church, Sant Miquel
de Montmell

Cross the dirt track diagonally to the right and continue uphill. At the path junction with a signpost go left to Església St Miquel XII (600m). Shortly after at the junction, go right and climb to the 12th-century church, **Sant Miquel de Montmell**.

Perched on rocks at 781m, the small Romanesque church, **Sant Miquel de Montmell**, was built near Montmell Castle. The castle dates back to AD976. However, the church was most probably built in the late 12th century. The new church of Sant Miquel was to replace the old church and was built at 640m, for easier access, in the 16th century. There are some remains of a small settlement around the church.

The Església Nova Sant Miquel is visible down below and you can also enjoy some great views towards the Montmell ridge stretching into the distance. From the church continue uphill. Occasionally you might have to use your hands as you climb this narrow rocky path. Ignore a path on the right and look out for green/white marks on the rocks. When the path splits, go left (the path on the right goes to Creu del Cap, a cross on the opposite mountain top) and about 20min from the old church arrive at the ruins of **Castell del Montmell**. From the top there are amazing views of Joncosa and a patchwork of vineyards, and the ridgeline leads the eye all the way to Tarragona on the coast.

From the ruins retrace your steps to the junction with a signpost just below the old church and go left towards *área recreativa* (picnic site). About 60 metres later leave this trail to the right on a path that descends to the dirt track below. Go right on the dirt track and follow it for 350 metres and when it widens, look out for a path on the left. Notice some purple marks painted on the rocks. After a steep climb reach the ridge.

Follow the ridge with some great views towards the village encircled by vineyards and mountains. The castle and church are behind you as you make your way along the ridge. Follow the undulating path among shrubs. You might notice another path to the left that goes to a flagpole – ignore this and continue on the ridge. There are some pines as you descend slightly. Go beneath an electricity wire and at the junction in a small col go right, and then keep slightly left on the path marked with a blue painted sign. Shortly after ascend again as you pass below **Puig de Migdia**. Follow the blue painted marks along the ridge with some great views of vineyards and hills all the way to the sea. The path bends left downhill as you descend on the rocky path.

About an hour after joining the path on the ridge, just below **Roca de l'Àliga**, the path splits; go left and notice a painted blue circle on a rock. There are views of the village and of the ridge that you traversed. Descend on rocks and through shrubs and then among pines. When the narrow path splits go left on the path with a painted blue sign and then left again towards the ruins. Pass the ruined farmhouse (**Mas Murat**) and at a junction, go right. Follow that track all the way to the tarmac road. Turn left and follow the tarmac road back to the village of **La Joncosa del Montmell** (10min).

APPENDIX A
Route summary table

Walk		Start/Finish	Route	Distance	Time	Ascent/Descent	Grade	Page
1	Turó de l'Home	Santa Fe	circular	11.5km	4hr	610m	2	25
2	Turó de Morou	Santa Fe	circular	6.5km	2hr	270m	1	28
3	Gualba to Santa Fe	Gualba to Santa Fe	linear	9.5km	3hr 30min–4hr	1060m/100m	3	31
4	Marianegra waterfall	Area de Les Ferreres	circular	11.5km	3hr 30min–4hr	560m	2	36
5	Les Agudes	Area de Les Ferreres	circular	8.5km/8km	4hr	600m	3/3+	41
6	Matagalls	Coll de Bordoriol	circular	10km	3hr 30min–4hr	650m	2	45
7	Sant Bernat/Sant Marçal	Hotel Sant Bernat	circular	12km	5hr–5hr 30min	810m	3	49
8	Aiguafreda	Aiguafreda	circular	16km	4hr 30min	420m	2	54
9	Matagalls	Collformic	circular	11.5km	4hr–4hr 30min	730m	2	60
10	Matagalls	Viladrau	return	19.5km	6hr	1120m	3	64
11	Castell de Taradell	Taradell	circular	10km	3hr 30min	380m	1	71
12	Tavèrnoles to Sant Pere de Casserres	Tavèrnoles to Sant Pere de Casserres	linear	11km/8km	3hr 30min–4hr/3hr–3hr 30min	390m/480m, 290m/440m	2	76
13	Puig del Far	Vilanova de Sau	circular	8km	3hr	350m	1	81
14	Pont de Malafogassa	Vilanova de Sau	return	7km	2hr–2hr 30min	190m	1	85

Walk	Start/Finish	Route	Distance	Time	Ascent/Descent	Grade	Page
15	Tavertet	circular	11km	4hr 30min–5hr	880m	3	88
16	Sant Miquel del Fai	circular	7km	2hr 30min	610m	1	95
17	Marquet de les Roques	circular	9km	4hr	650m	3	99
18	Matadepera	circular	8.5km	3hr–3hr 30min	500m	2	103
19	Torre de l'Àngel	circular	10.5km	3hr 30min	570m	2	108
20	Alzina del Salari	circular	8km	2hr 30min–3hr	440m	2	112
21	Coll d'Estenalles to Mura	linear	9km	3hr	100m/510m	1	116
22	Monistrol de Montserrat	circular	8.5km	3hr	670m	2	123
23	Monastir de Montserrat	circular	10.5km	3hr 30min–4hr	680m	3	128
24	Monastir de Montserrat	circular	6.5km	2hr 30min	600m	2	132
25	Coll Can Maçana	circular	9km	3hr 30min–4hr	850m	3	136
26	Coll Can Maçana	circular	8km	2hr 30min	330m	3	141
27	Collbató	return	12km	4hr–4hr 30min	700m	2	145
28	Garraf to Bruguers	linear	16km	4hr 30min–5hr	780m/500m	2	151
29	Jafra	circular	9km	2hr 30min–3hr	200m	1	157
30	Castellet	circular	28km	8hr–9hr	700m	3	160
31	Santuari de Foix	circular	9.5km	3hr–3hr 30min	300m	2	169
32	La Joncosa del Montmell	circular	9km	3hr–3hr 30min	490m	2	173

APPENDIX B
Useful contacts and information

Tourist information

www.catalunya.com

https://experience.catalunya.com

www.turismevalles.com

www.osonaturisme.cat

www.bagesturisme.cat

www.penedesturisme.cat

www.femturisme.cat

www.garrafturisme.cat

www.turisme-montseny.com

www.montserratvisita.com

https://parcs.diba.cat

Tourist information centres

Montseny
Espai Montseny visitor centre and
tourist information
Carrer del Migdia, 1,
Viladrau 17406,
Girona
tel +34938848035

Can Casades tourist information
BV-5114, Km, 21,
Santa Fe del 08479,
Barcelona
tel +34938475113

Montseny tourist information
Plaça Montseny, 9,
Montseny 08469,
Barcelona
tel +34938473137

Vic-Guilleries-Savassona
Vic tourist information
Plaça del Pes, s/n,
Vic 08500,
Barcelona
tel +34938862091

Tavertet tourist information
Jaume Balmes, 1,
Tavertet 08511
tel +34938565079

Sant Llorençe del Munt i l'Obac Natural Park
Coll d'Estenyalles tourist information
Ctra. de Terrassa a Navarcle, Km 14.8,
Mura 08230,
Barcelona
tel +34938317300

Mura tourist information
Pl. de l'Ajuntament, s/n,
Sant Fruitós de Bages 08278,
Barcelona
tel +34938318375

Montserrat
Montserrat tourist information
Monestir de Montserrat 08199,
Barcelona
tel +34938777701

Coll Can Maçana tourist information
Coll Can Maçana,
El Bruc 08294,
Barcelona
tel +34606747220

Penedès and Garraf
Vilafranca del Penedès tourist
information
Carrer Hermenegild Clascar, 2,
Vilafranca del Penedès 08720,
Barcelona
tel +34938181254

Sitges tourist information
Plaça Eduard Maristany, 2,
Sitges 08870,
Barcelona
tel +34938944251

Transport

Air
www.britishairways.com

www.vueling.com

www.easyjet.com

www.ryanair.com

www.skyscanner.net

Train
www.renfe.com

Bus
Teisa-intercity bus service
www.teisa-bus.com

Tmb-public transport Barcelona city
and surrounding area
www.tmb.cat

Car rental
www.rentalcars.com

www.holidayautos.com

www.avis.com

www.autoeurope.com

www.centauro.net

www.goldcar.es

www.europecar.com

www.hertz.com

www.budget.com

www.sixt.com

APPENDIX C
Accommodation

www.catalunya.com

www.booking.com

www.expedia.com

www.trivago.com

www.travelsupermarket.com

www.airbnb.co.uk

Rural tourism
http://establimentsturistics.gencat.cat

Campsites

Montseny
Masia Can Cervera
Carretera BV 5301, Km 15,
Montseny 08460,
Barcelona
tel +34938473066
www.cancervera.com

Càmping de Fontmartina
Carretera, BV-5119, Km 10,
La Costa de Montseny 08479,
Barcelona
tel +34938475163
www.fontmartina.cat

Càmping Les Piscines de Montseny
Carretera de Sta Ma. de Palautordera a
Montseny, Km 12.3,
Montseny 08460,
Barcelona
tel +34938473070
www.piscinesmontseny.com

Les Illes
Ctra. Sta Ma. de Palautordera – Seva,
Km 20,
Montseny 08469,
Barcelona
tel +34938473204
www.lesillesmontseny.es

Càmping del Parc Gualba
Parc Mediambiental Gualba, Can Illa
Vell, s/n,
Gualba 08474,
Barcelona
tel +34938487994
www.parcdegualba.cat/camping

Vic-Guilleries-Savassona Natural Area
Càmping La Vall
Camí la Vallmitjana, s/n,
Taradell 08552,
Barcelona
tel +34938126336
www.campinglavall.com

Càmping El Pont
S N, Complejo Camping El Pont,
Vilanova de Sau (Osona) 08519,
Barcelona
tel +34937430100
www.campingelpont.net

Santa Eugènia Park
Urbanització Creu del Cim,
Santa Eugènia de Berga 08507,
Barcelona
tel +34938853256
www.campingsantaeugeniapark.cat

Sant Llorenç del Munt i l'Obac Natural Park

Càmping El Pasqualet
Carretera BV-1243,
Caldes de Montbui 08140,
Barcelona
tel +34938654695
www.elpasqualet.com

Càmping La Tatgera
BV-1221,
Talamanca 08278,
Barcelona
tel +34647584526
https://campingtalamanca.com

Montserrat

Oller del Mas (Camping option is on request only)
Carretera de Igualada C37Z, Km 91,
Manresa 08241,
Barcelona
tel +34938768315
www.ollerdelmas.com

Càmping Freixa
Cami del Grau,
Manresa 08243,
Barcelona
tel +34938362799
www.campingfreixa.com

Penedès and Garraf

Vilanova Park
Ctra Arboç BV-2115, Km 2.5,
Vilanova i la Geltrú 08800,
Barcelona
tel +34938933402
www.vilanovapark.com

Càmping Tres Estrellas – Gavà
C-31, Km 186.2,
Gavà 08850,
Barcelona
tel +34936330637
www.tresestrellascampings.com/barcelona

Càmping El Garrofer
C-246a, Km 39,
Sitges 08870,
Barcelona
tel +34938941780
www.campingelgarrofer.com

APPENDIX D
Glossary

Catalan	Spanish	English
Greetings		
hola	*hola*	hello
Travel		
autobús	*autobús*	bus
bitllet	*billete*	ticket
cotxe	*coche*	car
estació d'autobusos	*estación de autobúses*	bus station
estació de tren	*estación de tren*	railway station
horaris	*horarios*	timetable
parada d'autobús	*parada de autobús*	bus stop
tren	*tren*	train
Accommodation		
autocaravana	*caravana*	campervan
càmping	*cámping*	campsite
habitació	*habitación*	room
tenda	*tienda*	tent
turisme rural	*turismo rural*	rural tourism
Animals		
abelles	*abejas*	bees
gosso	*perro*	dog
vaca	*vasa*	cow
In the town		
ajuntament	*ayuntamiento*	town hall
capella	*capilla*	chapel
carrer	*calle*	street
carretera	*carretera*	road

Catalan	Spanish	English
casa	*casa*	house
castell	*castillo*	castle
escola	*escuela*	school
església	*iglesia*	church
masia	*granja*	farmhouse
mercat	*mercado*	market
monastir	*monasterio*	monastery
obert	*abierto*	open
oficina de turisme	*oficina de turismo*	tourist office
supermercat	*supermercado*	supermarket
tancat	*cerrado*	closed
Food and drink		
aigua	*agua*	water
bebent aigua	*agua potable*	drinking water
dinar	*almuerzo*	lunch
esmorzar	*desayuno*	breakfast
sopar	*cena*	dinner
vi	*vino*	wine
On the trail		
àrea d'esplai	*área de recreo*	recreation area
avenc	*sima*	chasm
bosc	*bosque*	forest
cim	*cima*	summit
coll	*coll*	coll
cova	*cueva*	cave
elevació	*elevación*	elevation
entrada	*entrada*	entrance
excursionista	*excursionista*	hiker
font	*fuente*	spring

Catalan	Spanish	English
gorg, barranc	*barranco*	ravine
mapa	*mapa*	map
mina	*mina*	mine
muntanya	*montaña*	mountain
pantà, embassament	*embalse*	reservoir
parc natural	*parque natural*	natural park
perill	*peligro*	danger
pont	*puente*	bridge
presa	*represa*	dam
privat	*privado*	private
puig	*pico*	peak
riu, riera	*río*	river
roca	*roca*	rock
ruta, recorregud	*ruta, recorrido*	route
salida	*sortida*	exit
salt, cascada	*cascada*	waterfall
sendero, camí	*sendero, camino*	trail, path
torrent, sot	*torrente*	stream
turó	*cerro*	hill
vall	*valle*	valley
Emergencies		
ambulància	*ambulancia*	ambulance
bombers	*bomberos*	fire brigade
emergència	*emergencia*	emergency
foc	*fuego*	fire
policia	*policía*	police

NOTES

The unobstructed panorama from Sant Jeroni is dominated by jagged peaks (Walk 23)

DOWNLOAD THE ROUTES
IN GPX FORMAT

All the routes in this guide are available for download from:

www.cicerone.co.uk/1077/GPX

as standard format GPX files. You should be able to load them into most online GPX systems and mobile devices, whether GPS or smartphone. You may need to convert the file into your preferred format using a conversion programme such as gpsvisualizer.com or one of the many other such websites and programmes.

When you follow this link, you will be asked for your email address and where you purchased the guidebook, and have the option to subscribe to the Cicerone e-newsletter.

www.cicerone.co.uk

LISTING OF CICERONE GUIDES

BRITISH ISLES CHALLENGES, COLLECTIONS AND ACTIVITIES

Cycling Land's End to John o' Groats
Great Walks on the England Coast Path
The Big Rounds
The Book of the Bivvy
The Book of the Bothy
The Mountains of England & Wales:
  Vol 1 Wales
  Vol 2 England
The National Trails
Walking The End to End Trail

SCOTLAND

Ben Nevis and Glen Coe
Cycle Touring in Northern Scotland
Cycling in the Hebrides
Great Mountain Days in Scotland
Mountain Biking in Southern and Central Scotland
Mountain Biking in West and North West Scotland
Not the West Highland Way
Scotland
Scotland's Mountain Ridges
Scottish Wild Country Backpacking
Skye's Cuillin Ridge Traverse
The Borders Abbeys Way
The Great Glen Way
The Great Glen Way Map Booklet
The Hebridean Way
The Hebrides
The Isle of Mull
The Isle of Skye
The Skye Trail
The Southern Upland Way
The Speyside Way
The Speyside Way Map Booklet
The West Highland Way
The West Highland Way Map Booklet
Walking Ben Lawers, Rannoch and Atholl
Walking in the Cairngorms
Walking in the Pentland Hills
Walking in the Scottish Borders
Walking in the Southern Uplands
Walking in Torridon, Fisherfield, Fannichs and An Teallach
Walking Loch Lomond and the Trossachs
Walking on Arran
Walking on Harris and Lewis
Walking on Jura, Islay and Colonsay
Walking on Rum and the Small Isles
Walking on the Orkney and Shetland Isles
Walking on Uist and Barra
Walking the Cape Wrath Trail

Walking the Corbetts
  Vol 1 South of the Great Glen
  Vol 2 North of the Great Glen
Walking the Galloway Hills
Walking the Munros
  Vol 1 – Southern, Central and Western Highlands
  Vol 2 – Northern Highlands and the Cairngorms
Winter Climbs Ben Nevis and Glen Coe

NORTHERN ENGLAND ROUTES

Cycling the Reivers Route
Cycling the Way of the Roses
Hadrian's Cycleway
Hadrian's Wall Path
Hadrian's Wall Path Map Booklet
The C2C Cycle Route
The Coast to Coast Map Booklet
The Coast to Coast Walk
The Pennine Way
The Pennine Way Map Booklet
Walking the Dales Way
Walking the Dales Way Map Booklet

NORTH-EAST ENGLAND, YORKSHIRE DALES AND PENNINES

Cycling in the Yorkshire Dales
Great Mountain Days in the Pennines
Mountain Biking in the Yorkshire Dales
St Oswald's Way and St Cuthbert's Way
The Cleveland Way and the Yorkshire Wolds Way
The Cleveland Way Map Booklet
The North York Moors
The Reivers Way
Trail and Fell Running in the Yorkshire Dales
Walking in County Durham
Walking in Northumberland
Walking in the North Pennines
Walking in the Yorkshire Dales: North and East
Walking in the Yorkshire Dales: South and West

NORTH-WEST ENGLAND AND THE ISLE OF MAN

Cycling the Pennine Bridleway
Isle of Man Coastal Path
The Lancashire Cycleway
The Lune Valley and Howgills
Walking in Cumbria's Eden Valley
Walking in Lancashire

Walking in the Forest of Bowland and Pendle
Walking on the Isle of Man
Walking on the West Pennine Moors
Walks in Silverdale and Arnside

LAKE DISTRICT

Cycling in the Lake District
Great Mountain Days in the Lake District
Joss Naylor's Lakes, Meres and Waters of the Lake District
Lake District Winter Climbs
Lake District: High Level and Fell Walks
Lake District: Low Level and Lake Walks
Mountain Biking in the Lake District
Outdoor Adventures with Children – Lake District
Scrambles in the Lake District – North
Scrambles in the Lake District – South
Trail and Fell Running in the Lake District
Walking The Cumbria Way
Walking the Lake District Fells –
  Borrowdale
  Buttermere
  Coniston
  Keswick
  Langdale
  Mardale and the Far East
  Patterdale
  Wasdale
Walking the Tour of the Lake District

DERBYSHIRE, PEAK DISTRICT AND MIDLANDS

Cycling in the Peak District
Dark Peak Walks
Scrambles in the Dark Peak
Walking in Derbyshire
Walking in the Peak District – White Peak East
Walking in the Peak District – White Peak West

SOUTHERN ENGLAND

20 Classic Sportive Rides in South East England
20 Classic Sportive Rides in South West England
Cycling in the Cotswolds
Mountain Biking on the North Downs
Mountain Biking on the South Downs

For full information on all our guides, books and eBooks, visit our website:
www.cicerone.co.uk

CICERONE

Trust Cicerone to guide your next adventure,
wherever it may be around the world...

Discover guides for hiking, mountain walking, backpacking,
trekking, trail running, cycling and mountain biking, ski touring,
climbing and scrambling in Britain, Europe and worldwide.

Connect with Cicerone online and find inspiration.

- buy books and ebooks
- articles, advice and trip reports
- podcasts and live events
- GPX files and updates
- regular newsletter

cicerone.co.uk